The
Theory of
Microeconomic
Policy

The Theory of Microeconomic Policy

Nancy Smith Barrett
The American University

D. C. HEATH AND COMPANY
Lexington, Massachusetts   Toronto   London

To My Mother and Father

PREFACE

Microeconomic theory in the United States has been heavily dominated by the laissez faire tradition of Adam Smith. The classical and neoclassical models of a capitalist economy that purport to demonstrate how the invisible hand of the market produces the most socially desirable allocation of resources have confused the debate over appropriate public policy actions. Although Keynesian economics has produced a generally accepted view that government has a role in regulating *aggregate* demand, there is still concern that government interference *within markets* has undesirable effects. Thus, despite the acknowledged breakdown of a market system in the face of external factors (air pollution, interdependent tastes), economies of scale, and the provision of public goods, microeconomic theory texts generally deal with how a market system operates rather than with what can be done to make it operate better.

In addition to avoiding policy issues the traditional approach is to begin with a discussion of the behavior of households and firms, which leaves most readers bewildered. Who cares what households and firms do? This book starts where most others end—with an examination of the underlying problem facing all economic systems: the need to allocate scarce resources as efficiently as possible. The discussion of resource allocation in chapters 1 and 2 is abstracted from any particular institutional context. In chapters 3 and 4 the market model and the Lange model of decentralized socialism are discussed and compared as institutional models that are supposed to produce efficient resource allocation. Once the allocative problem is put into perspective, the question of appropriate public policies follows naturally.

Later chapters provide the analytical framework for the study of resource allocation and the requisite tools for analyzing practical problems and policy issues. In addition to the standard neoclassical paradigm a number of contemporary topics are considered, including behavior under uncertainty, linear programming and duality, input-output analysis, behavioral theories of the firm, and stability analysis. An entire chapter is devoted to capital theory and resource allocation over time.

This book is designed for a course in microeconomic theory beyond the introductory level. No mathematics beyond elementary algebra is required.

Nancy Smith Barrett

CONTENTS

part **I**
THE THEORY OF EFFICIENT RESOURCE ALLOCATION

1   **Microeconomic Theory and Economic Policy**   3

    1–1   Basic Propositions of Microeconomics   3
    1–2   Perspectives of Microeconomic Theory   5
    1–3   The Laissez-Faire Tradition   5
    1–4   Microeconomic Theory and the Keynesian Revolution   7
    1–5   Microeconomic Policy in a Market System   8
    1–6   Microeconomic Policy Instead of a Market System   9
    1–7   Methodological Framework: Economic Models   10

2   **Resource Allocation and Economic Efficiency**   13

    2–1   A Digression on Scarcity   14
    2–2   Criteria for Optimal Resource Allocation   15
    2–3   Conditions for Pareto Optimality   20
    2–4   The Marginal Conditions and Economic Efficiency   35

3   **Economic Efficiency in a Market System**   37

    3–1   The Theoretical Justification for Markets   37
    3–2   Market Failures   42
    3–3   The Theory of Second Best   56
    3–4   Taxation and Economic Efficiency   58

4   **Alternative Economic Systems**   62

    4–1   Resource Allocation Outside the Market   62
    4–2   Central Planning: The Target Approach   64
    4–3   Prices and Economic Efficiency   65
    4–4   The Lange Model of Competitive Socialism   66
    4–5   Evaluation of the Lange Model   70
    4–6   The Market and Nonmarket Models Compared   71
    4–7   Nonmarket Decisions in a Market Economy   73

part II
TOOLS OF ANALYSIS

5   The Household Sector   79

5-1   The Classical Approach   79
5-2   The Indifference Analysis   91
5-3   Classical and Indifference Analyses Compared   104
5-4   Deriving a Utility Function from an Indifference Map   109
5-5   The Supply of Labor   110
5-6   Revealed Preference   113

6   The Theory of Production   119

6-1   Technology and Optimization in Production   119
6-2   Cost Curves and Production Functions   136
6-3   Transformation of Commodities   140
6-4   Profit Maximization and the Supply Curve for the Firm   148
6-5   Technological Change   151

7   Productivity and Distribution   157

7-1   The Marginal Productivity Principle   157
7-2   Factor Supply and Distribution   162
7-3   The Theory of Rent   167
7-4   The Product Exhaustion Theorem   170
7-5   Factor Shares and the Production Function   173
7-6   Evaluation of the Marginal Productivity Principle of Distribution   177

8   Market Equilibrium   179

8-1   The Concept of Market Equilibrium   180
8-2   Comparative Statics and the Correspondence Principle   182
8-3   Equilibrium in Product and Factor Markets   184
8-4   Stability Analysis   192
8-5   General Equilibrium   199

part III
BEYOND THE STATIC COMPETITIVE MODEL   209

9   Market Structure and Performance   211

9-1   The Structure of American Industry   212
9-2   Determinants of Industrial Concentration   212
9-3   Market Structure and Market Performance   220
9-4   Duopoly and Oligopoly   231
9-5   Monopolistic Competition   245

9–6   The Impact of Market Structure on Factor Pricing and Employment   248

10   Resource Allocation over Time   257

10–1   Allocative Efficiency over Time   257
10–2   Capital as a Factor of Production   258
10–3   Capital Productivity and the Internal Rate of Return   261
10–4   Investment Criteria and the Optimal Rate of Investment   266
10–5   The Rate of Time Preference   273
10–6   Determination of the Rate of Interest   277
10–7   Planning for Intertemporal Efficiency   281

11   Welfare Economics   284

11–1   Efficiency Criteria   284
11–2   Distributional Criteria   291
11–3   Special Problems in Welfare Economics   297
11–4   The Theory of Microeconomic Policy: A Summing Up   299

Index   303

part **I**

THE THEORY OF EFFICIENT
RESOURCE ALLOCATION

1 Microeconomic Theory and Economic Policy

One sure way to start an argument among a group of economists is to ask for a definition of economics. Perhaps the only point of agreement would be that economics has to do with scarcity. If resources and hence the goods and services produced were unlimited, there would be nothing to economize. Therefore, it is the limitation of resources that gives rise to the "economic problem."

Some economists view economics as the theory of rational choice between mutually exclusive alternatives.[1] Others have defined it as the theory of optimization subject to certain limitations, or constraints.[2] Still others view economics as a study of the behavior of individuals seeking to maximize their material satisfaction given limited resources.[3]

1-1 BASIC PROPOSITIONS OF MICROECONOMICS

This book is about the allocation of economic, or scarce, resources. When resources are scarce, goods and services are scarce and society develops (consciously or unconsciously) a system to determine how to use the resources to produce goods and services, what goods and services to produce, and how to ration these goods and services among its members. Such a system is called an **economic system.** Although different societies may have different values, and although they may develop different sorts of institutions to achieve their objectives, there are some basic propositions that any society economizing scarce resources must accept.

1. *Scarce resources should not be left idle.*

Clearly, if resources are scarce, then involuntary unemployment of

---

[1] For instance, see Oskar Lange, *On the Economic Theory of Socialism* (Minneapolis: University of Minnesota Press, 1938), pp. 59ff., and Vivian Charles Walsh, *Introduction to Contemporary Microeconomics* (New York: McGraw-Hill, 1970).

[2] For instance, see Paul A. Samuelson, *Foundations of Economic Analysis* (Cambridge, Mass.: Harvard University Press, 1947).

[3] For instance, see Alfred Marshall, *Principles of Economics* (London: Macmillan and Co., Ltd., 1959). This book was first published in 1890.

these resources is wasteful. When scarce resources are not put to some use, then the economic system is not realizing its full productive potential. This does not imply that we all must work sixteen hours a day. Leisure as well as labor is scarce. Full utilization of labor resources implies that if a person *wants* to work (that is, if he prefers work to leisure at the prevailing wage), he should be able to find a job. Furthermore, useful capital equipment that is not technologically obsolete should not lie idle. However, this does not mean that all machines must be run continuously without shutdowns for maintenance. There is an optimal rate of utilization of capital equipment as well as labor. Machines that are run too hard may wear out much faster than those allowed shutdown periods. Consequently, full employment of resources means that the labor force and the capital stock should be used at some optimal rate, not necessarily that they be used to maximum capacity.

2. *The optimal technology for producing a good or service is that which uses the least resources.*

A technique that uses three man-days of labor is preferred to one using four man-days of labor when the outputs of the techniques are identical. Equivalently, from a given resource input, more is better than less. By the first technique, twelve man-days of labor can produce one and one-third times the output obtained by using the second technique.

Using resources in less productive techniques than are currently available is often called hidden unemployment. In our example, the use of a less productive technique gives the same output as if a more productive technique were used and one out of every four persons were involuntarily unemployed. If the more efficient technique were introduced into the industry, additional resources would be released to increase output in that industry or in other sectors of the economy.

3. *If someone can be made better off without making someone else worse off, the change would represent an improvement.*

Clearly, if some people can gain from a change without hurting others, the change would be considered an improvement by all concerned. Of course, those who have gained little or not at all may resent the greater gains by others as a result of the change. If such resentment actually makes these people worse off, then we cannot say that no one has been hurt by the change. In determining the effect of any change in resource allocation on the welfare of individuals, all interactions must be accounted for. Modern economic theory recognizes that individual welfare may depend as much upon relative levels of material consumption as upon absolute levels.

An individual society will have other economic goals. Some countries may be concerned with equitable distribution of income, others with rapid growth or the development of a strong military establishment. But the criteria just listed are consistent with any of these specific objectives. These criteria must be observed if scarce resources are to put to their best use, however that concept is defined.

1–2   PERSPECTIVES OF MICROECONOMIC THEORY

Microeconomics, the study of resource allocation, has three major perspectives:

1. *Microeconomics describes the behavior of economic units.*

By analyzing how individual households and firms make choices in the face of scarcity, microeconomics can predict how they will react to changes in conditions that affect their choice between economic alternatives. How will an excise tax on automobiles affect car sales? Will manufacturers pass on a sales tax to consumers? How will a rising trend in real wages affect labor force participation of married women? What fiscal measures would cause polluting industries to switch to cleaner processes?

2. *Microeconomics develops criteria for optimal resource allocation.*

Given certain objectives with known constraints (or scarcities), what are the rules that must be followed if the optimum is to be achieved? Such an analysis has implications for any decision maker concerned with resource allocation — in business, government, a large corporation, or the central planning board of a socialist state. A labor union trying to maximize incomes of its members, an airline that wants to minimize the cost of flying a particular schedule, a household that wants to get the most nutrition from its food budget can all utilize the principles of microeconomic theory.

3. *Microeconomics can be used to evaluate behavior and economic institutions.*

Although historically microeconomics has been developed largely in reference to a market system, its concepts may easily be applied in discussing the problems of resource allocation in any society. Microeconomics is useful for evaluating alternative institutions and economic policies that a society might devise for achieving optimal resource allocation. For instance, what is the best way to achieve efficient urban transportation? Should college education be financed by individuals or the state? How can we deal most effectively with the massive economies of scale that characterize modern industrial technology?

1–3   THE LAISSEZ FAIRE TRADITION

An approach that combines an exposition of microeconomic theory with matters of economic policy may, at first glance, appear to be a misguided effort, flying in the face of the laissez faire tradition that has pervaded economics for two centuries. The idea that a free market with a minimum of interference from government is the best mode of resource allocation rests largely on the doctrine of the invisible hand set forth by Adam Smith in 1776 in *The Wealth of Nations.* Smith stated:

> Every individual is continually exerting himself to find out the most advantageous employment for whatever capital he can command. It is his own

> advantage, indeed, and not that of the society, which he has in view. But the study of his own advantage naturally, or rather necessarily, leads him to prefer that employment which is most advantageous to the society.[4]

The notion that individuals acting in self-interest achieve an optimal allocation of economic (scarce) resources from the point of view of society as a whole led naturally to the conclusion that no outside arbiter such as the central government should interfere with individual choices. This resulted in the enunciation of the laissez faire principle:

> No regulation of commerce can increase the quantity of industry in any society beyond what its capital can maintain. It can only divert a part of it into a direction into which it might not otherwise have gone; and it is by no means certain that this artificial direction is likely to be more advantageous to the society than that into which it would have gone of its own accord.[5]

Economic theory since Smith has largely been concerned with showing the conditions under which a laissez faire policy (or more appropriately, nonpolicy) will result in a socially optimal allocation of resources. Economic policy has, for the most part, been aimed at establishing these preconditions. Antitrust legislation, advocacy of free trade, measures to improve labor and capital mobility are all examples of economic policies consistent with the laissez faire approach to resource allocation. That is, these policies are designed to structure economic institutions so that optimal resource allocation will occur in the absence of direct government intervention. Some classical liberals like Milton Friedman have gone so far as to advocate the abolition of minimum wage laws and provisions prohibiting job discrimination.[6]

However, economists have also recognized areas in which a free enterprise system fails to provide the most desirable allocation of resources. Air pollution, poverty, excessive concentrations of economic power (and hence political power) in huge corporations and labor unions are all examples of some undesirable results of laissez faire attitudes. Yet the laissez faire tradition dominates thinking in the area of resource allocation. The antitrust division of the Department of Justice still prosecutes monopolies with a vengeance, on the assumption that breaking a single corporate giant into two or three corporate giants will somehow benefit consumers. Much of the controversy over wage-price controls to alleviate inflation centers on whether such controls would interfere with "free market forces."

Such policies and controversies are anomalies indeed, pursued as they are in an environment that is quite obviously in violation of the preconditions set forth by traditional economic theory for optimal resource allocation. Not only is American industry not perfectly competitive but economic theory cites many instances

---

[4] Adam Smith, *The Wealth of Nations* (New York: Random House, 1937), p. 421.

[5] Ibid.

[6] Milton Friedman, *Capitalism and Freedom* (Chicago: University of Chicago Press, 1962), chapter 7.

in which even a perfectly competitive economy will not produce a socially optimal resource allocation. Thus, although economic theory leads us to support
laissez faire policies in some instances, it can also provide a guide for economic
policy when laissez faire is clearly not advantageous.

Although economic theory has been used to justify free market capitalism, it
can be shown that there are alternative economic systems that can also produce
a desirable allocation of resources. Central planning, for instance, can sometimes be designed to achieve what a market system fails to do. Various economic
systems have their strengths and weaknesses, which can be evaluated, in part,
using the principles of microeconomic theory.

1-4 MICROECONOMIC THEORY AND THE KEYNESIAN REVOLUTION

One of the most obvious historical failures of laissez faire to achieve optimal
resource allocation was the Great Depression of the 1930s. The Keynesian revo-
lution in economic theory, which followed on the heels of that depression,
clearly established a role for a public economic policy other than laissez faire.
After the publication of Keynes's *The General Theory of Employment, Interest,
and Money* it became acceptable for government to intervene in the economy to
promote full employment. This intervention, however, was to be strictly on the
"aggregate" level, that is, it was not to interfere with the market mechanism. However, it is unlikely that the public sector can be expected to expropriate ever
larger portions of the national product in the name of functional finance or economic stabilization without interfering with the allocation of resources by the
private sector. Furthermore, in the United States, as public spending rose from 10
per cent of GNP in 1929 to 31 per cent in 1969, the allocation of an increasing
portion of the nation's resources was taking place outside the market system.
Although Keynes foresaw the inevitability of the public sector growing more
rapidly than the economy as a whole, he failed to consider the consequences for
the allocation of resources among alternative uses. During the Great Depression,
when he wrote *General Theory*, a substantial portion of the nation's resources
were unemployed and any enterprise, regardless of its social worth, was prefer-
able to leaving those resources idle.

> . . . if the Treasury were to fill old bottles with banknotes, bury them at
> suitable depths in disused coal mines which are then filled up to the surface
> with town rubbish, and leave it to private enterprise on well-tried principles
> of *laissez-faire* to dig the notes up again . . . , there need be no more unem-
> ployment and, with the help of the repercussions, the real income of the
> community and its capital wealth also, would probably become a good deal
> greater than it actually is.[7]

---

[7] John Maynard Keynes, *The General Theory of Employment, Interest, and Money* (New York: Har-
court Brace Jovanovich, 1965), p. 129.

He also suggested that endeavors of little use value, such as pyramid building and the erection of cathedrals, would be sure to generate full employment, since the populace would never complain of having too many of them. "Two pyramids, two masses for the dead, are twice as good as one; but not so two railways from London to York."[8]

One thing that Keynes failed to recognize is the irreversibility of public spending programs once they are initiated. The idea that spending for the sake of spending is a good thing presents serious questions for resource allocation in a full employment economy. What happens when the Office of Pyramid Construction develops such economic and political power that it wins increasingly large budgetary appropriations from the Congress at the expense of education, medical care, and other endeavors with obvious social merit?[9]

Basically, however, in establishing an active role for government in the economy, Keynesian economics has resulted in nearly one third of United States GNP being purchased by the government. Decisions concerning what, how, and for whom goods and services are produced are made outside a market system.

An analogy can be made with the large corporation—the dominant type of producer in the manufacturing sector of the American economy in terms of value added in production. These corporations often produce their own input (or dominate the sources of supply), service their own products, and control large pools of specialized labor. The decisions concerning how to allocate resources among alternative product lines must often be made in the absence of market criteria such as prices.

Lange once noted that optimal decisions cannot be made without knowing the terms on which alternatives are offered.[10] This proposition is the key to understanding how microeconomic theory can guide optimal decision making in the absence of a market. Put in another way, the laissez faire principle states that under certain conditions a free market system (with no government interference) produces an optimal allocation of resources. However, microeconomics is a way to analyze economic options in the absence of market information. Furthermore, it can indicate when a free market system is likely to fail to provide the optimal institutional framework.

1-5   MICROECONOMIC POLICY IN A MARKET SYSTEM

Microeconomic policy is important for a market system in two types of circumstances. The first is the case of market failures, that is, when a free market economy fails to produce optimal resource allocation. The second is where large amounts of goods and services are allocated outside markets, that is, within and among large corporations and in the public sector.

---

[8] Ibid., p. 131.

[9] For further discussion see Nancy S. Barrett, The Theory of Macroeconomic Policy (Englewood Cliffs, N.J.: Prentice-Hall, 1972), pp. 338–339.

[10] Lange, Economic Theory of Socialism, p. 60.

From the time of Adam Smith traditional economic theory has recognized that there are certain areas in which private decisions will not produce socially desirable results. There are many instances where private interests differ from social interests. My decision to plant a garden will be based only on the satisfaction I expect to receive from the garden. But this private calculation will understate the benefit derived by the entire neighborhood from such an improvement. A petroleum refining company emitting sulfur oxides does not include such emissions in a calculation of its production costs, even though air pollution represents a *social* cost. Only to the extent that private and social costs and benefits coincide will laissez faire result in maximum social well-being.

Another area in which a laissez faire policy fails to solve society's economic problems is income distribution. Economists have traditionally treated the question of optimal income distribution as a normative one, that is, requiring individual value judgments. In other words, the question of whom goods should be produced for is regarded as having no scientific answer. However, it may be apparent that the distributive consequences of some particular action are not beneficial from the viewpoint of the bulk of society. Consider the case of a wealthy recluse living in the midst of a poor community. His estate lies in the path of the only access road to the market, and he exacts a toll from all those who use the road. Suppose the tolls are regulated by a government agency. Noting that the roads are congested, the recluse requests an increase in the tolls. His argument is that if the tolls rise, fewer people would use the road and consequently it wou'd be less congested. However, the agency in making its decision would certainly take the distributive consequences of such an action into account. An alternative might be to build a new road from revenues obtained by taxing the property of the wealthy recluse. In both cases, the allocative effect would be to reduce the traffic congestion and hence the cost of transportation to and from the market. The distributive consequences, however, would be quite different.

Finally, microeconomic policy is needed in a market economy when allocative decisions are made outside the market system. The growth of the public sector because of the growing demand for public goods and the acceptance of Keynesian principles of functional finance, and the growth of large corporations because of economies of scale and other advantages associated with size, has meant that many decisions concerning what, how, and for whom goods and services should be produced are made by people other than autonomous market participants. Microeconomic theory can provide criteria for resource allocation under those circumstances.

1–6 MICROECONOMIC POLICY INSTEAD OF A MARKET SYSTEM

Microeconomic theory can provide criteria for optimal resource allocation. Although the economic objectives of a society are related to its institutions, the notion of optimal resource allocation can be considered apart from the institutions a society develops to achieve its goals. Thus, given social objectives, microeconomics can be used to evaluate social institutions and policies designed to achieve those objectives. Furthermore, given certain objectives, theory would suggest the best policies to achieve those ends, with laissez faire being one possibility.

One example of how microeconomic theory can be used for economic decision making in a nonmarket setting is **benefit-cost analysis,** now widely used in government and industry. In many such studies values, or **shadow prices,** must be imputed to resources when market values are either not available or else assumed to be irrelevant because of the divergence of private and social returns. For instance, in determining an optimal rate of government investment, some economists advocate use of an interest rate (discount factor) that is lower than the market rate. This is because it is expected that society as a whole has a weaker preference for current consumption than individuals, because of the limited life-span of the latter. Thus society, including future generations, would generally prefer longer-lived investments and a higher level of investment (with less current consumption) than individuals of the present generation.

1-7 METHODOLOGICAL FRAMEWORK: ECONOMIC MODELS[11]

Economic theory involves formulating and describing hypotheses about economic behavior, recognizing interrelations among various aspects of economic behavior, and analyzing the implications of these interrelations. One way to examine the hypotheses and interrelations of economic theory is to construct a **model.**

A model distills the essence of the problem under investigation. It simplifies the analysis by stripping away the unnecessary assumptions and empirical details while retaining those needed to obtain useful insights and operational results. A test of the skill of a theoretician is his ability to simplify a complex problem.

Suppose we are interested in how price is determined in a particular market. A model of the market can be based upon certain hypotheses about market behavior as well as upon the interrelations between buyers and sellers in the market. Suppose we assume

1. The quantity of the good demanded is a linear function of its price, or algebraically,

$$q_D = a_1 + a_2 p$$

---

[11] The material in this section is largely taken from the introductory chapter of Barrett, *The Theory of Macroeconomic Policy.*

2. The quantity of the good supplied is also a linear function of its price, or

$$q_S = b_1 + b_2 p$$

3. Buyers and sellers will adjust their offering prices until the market is cleared, that is, until quantity demanded equals quantity supplied, or

$$q_D = q_S$$

The first two equations are **behavioral relations;** the third is an **equilibrium condition.**

A model must not only be simple but must also yield operational results, that is, it must be capable of providing answers to relevant questions. Suppose we want to predict market price on the basis of our model.

The complete model

$$q_D = a_1 + a_2 p$$
$$q_S = b_1 + b_2 p$$
$$q_D = q_S$$

has three equations and three unknowns. Consequently, it is consistent, that is, the equilibrium market price can be determined (except in special cases).[12]

In equilibrium

$$q_D = q_S$$

and substituting the behavioral relations for q_D and q_S, the equilibrium condition can be expressed as

$$a_1 + a_2 p = b_1 + b_2 p$$

Solving for p, the price in equilibrium is found to be

$$p = \frac{b_1 - a_1}{a_2 - b_2}$$

A model may be used to answer other questions. How does the market price fluctuate over time? What happens when the system is not in equilibrium? How would market price respond to an increase in demand? To answer these questions more information may be needed. However, the answers can all be found in the context of the model just presented.

Mathematics in Economic Models

A model of economic theory need not be mathematical; however, mathematics has several attributes that contribute to its usefulness in economic theorizing. First,

---

[12] The results should also be economically meaningful. In this case, equilibrium price and quantities demanded and supplied should be non-negative.

it provides a shorthand notation in which to express the variables of the model. Then, mathematics is a powerful tool of analysis that can contribute to problem solving in economics. Differential calculus, for instance, can provide techniques for optimization analysis, so important to questions of resource allocation.

Although mathematics is not the only tool for model building, it is an important one. However, it can only be used once the underlying economic relations of the model have been specified. The specification of a model, the development of behavioral hypotheses, and recognition of underlying relations are clearly the most challenging aspects of economic theory.

QUESTIONS FOR STUDY AND REVIEW

1. How can you explain the traditional association of microeconomic theory with laissez faire capitalism? Describe some other areas in which microeconomic theory can provide fruitful insights for economic policy.

2. What is the relevance of Keynesian (macro)economics to microeconomics? Of microeconomics to Keynesian (macroeconomic) theory?

3. "During World War II, resource allocation in the United States was at an all time optimum, since both the labor force and capital stock were being utilized to their maximum capacity." Discuss.

4. Discuss the model-building approach as a methodology in economic theory. Explain the statement in the text that the specification of a model is clearly the most challenging aspect of economic theory.

ADDITIONAL READING

Boulding, Kenneth E. "Economics as a Moral Science," *American Economic Review, LIX* (March 1969), pp. 1–12.

Friedman, Milton. *Essays in Positive Economics*. Chicago: University of Chicago Press, 1953, part I.

Heilbroner, Robert. *The Worldly Philosophers*. New York: Simon and Schuster, 1967, chapter 3.

Kuhn, Thomas S. *The Structure of Scientific Revolutions*. Chicago: University of Chicago Press, 1970.

2 Resource Allocation and Economic Efficiency

Scarcity is the basic problem facing economic science. Since resources and thus goods and services are scarce, it is clear that full utilization of these resources is an important goal of an economic system. However, full utilization alone does not ensure that resources are being used to their best advantage. A person may work fifteen hours per day making square wheels, while another works eight hours producing round ones. From the viewpoint of society, the use of the labor force resource producing round wheels for eight hours may be more beneficial than the fifteen-hour effort that produces square ones. Thus, even if resources are fully utilized, the question of *what* is produced is certainly relevant to the problem of scarcity.

Suppose a man spends eight hours producing a useful item such as round wheels, but a machine is available with which he can produce the same number of wheels in an hour. The labor-intensive method may prove to be a waste of resources, depending, of course, on the cost of the machine. Clearly, the question of *how* resources are used to produce goods and services is relevant to the problem of scarcity.

Finally, suppose there are two wagon makers in the economy. One has an excessive inventory of wheels, while the other has halted production because of a lack of wheels. Now suppose the wheel maker delivers his wheels to the wagon maker with an excessive inventory of wheels. Although he has expended his labor (a scarce resource) on a useful product, using an efficient technique, he has not lessened scarcity, since he has delivered his goods to a person who already has an abundance of that product. Consequently, the question of *for whom* goods and services are produced is also relevant to the question of scarcity.

Optimal resource allocation clearly involves more than the assurance that all resources are fully employed. They must also be used efficiently to produce useful goods and services that are distributed to individuals who want them. In this chapter we will consider the criteria economists use to determine when, in fact, optimal allocation of resources has been achieved. In other words, how does one know that scarce resources have been used to best advantage?

2-1   A DIGRESSION ON SCARCITY

Although the basic economic resources, labor, capital, and natural resources are available in limited amounts, the rates at which they are utilized can be varied. The notion of full employment is consistent with many rates of resource utilization, and a resource may be viewed as scarce even though it is not being used at its maximum potential.

The labor of each individual, for instance, is potentially available for twenty-four hours a day. However, use at that rate would be shortsighted, since human beings need rest, food, and recreation to maintain labor effectiveness for any length of time. Furthermore, individuals may prefer to consume leisure in the place of goods and services. Even though leisure is not technically produced, it uses resources (since it holds labor resources from production) and consequently must be viewed as an economic, or scarce, good. Thus resources voluntarily allocated to leisure cannot be viewed as unemployed.[1] Maximum labor force participation does not necessarily represent optimal resource allocation, since there may be inadequate allocation of resources to leisure.

Labor resources can be increased in ways other than reducing allocation to leisure. Women, children, and the elderly can all be called into service. Although this practice has been followed in times of national emergency, it does not necessarily represent an improved allocation of resources if individuals prefer to use their resources in endeavors such as child rearing, education, and recreation. It is a mistake to consider such activities as out of the sphere of economics, because they all involve the use of scarce resources. The allocation of time to activities outside the labor force is an important consideration for economic theory. As goods and services become increasingly abundant, it is likely that individuals will desire to spend less time producing them and more time in other activities. Consequently, this area of economic analysis is likely to increase in importance.

We have seen that the notion of full employment of labor must be viewed in terms of all potential uses of that resource. In addition, all labor force activity does not involve direct production of consumer goods and services. Some labor resources are transformed into another resource, capital, which is then used to produce other goods and services. Capital is a produced means of production. The question of how much labor to devote to producing capital is an important problem of resource allocation. Furthermore, the notion of full employment of capital is not as straightforward as it might seem.

General Electric invested millions of dollars in capital equipment to manufacture black and white television. With the advent of color television, some of the equipment was converted but much of it had to be scrapped and replaced with completely new machines. Was the scrapping of machinery that had not

---

[1] If workers are involuntarily unemployed, their consumption of leisure is involuntary and leisure, like excessive wheel inventories, is no longer a scarce commodity for those individuals.

outlived its productive service an uneconomic decision? Not necessarily. The optimal rate of replacement of machinery must be viewed in terms of technological advance as well as in relation to changes in demand for products. If demand for black and white television decreases, or if machines that can produce both black and white and color components are available, then machinery for producing only black and white components becomes a redundant resource, even though the labor resources that produced it are scarce. This does not violate the principle that scarce resources must be fully employed if they are to be allocated to the best advantage.

Finally, natural resources can be utilized at different rates without compromising the full employment principle. Although the total stock of many of the natural resources available to us and to future generations is fixed, the flow rate of utilization affects the rate of depletion. The trade-off between immediate and future use of a fixed stock of resources is again a question of resource allocation. For instance, many economists believe that governments should control the rate at which the present generation depletes natural resources, since the limited horizons of individuals undervalue future resource requirements. If these economists are correct, this is a case where laissez faire breaks down as means of optimal resource allocation because of the divergence of private interests (of the present generation) and the social interest (including that of future generations).

Thus full employment of resources cannot be defined in any one way. In fact, the question of the optimal rate of resource utilization or supply is one of the important issues of microeconomic theory and policy. We will return to that question in this and later chapters.

2–2 CRITERIA FOR OPTIMAL RESOURCE ALLOCATION

Designing a policy to produce optimal resource allocation presupposes certain social goals or objectives. Criteria by which alternative allocations can be ranked or evaluated are called **welfare criteria.** Welfare criteria can be used to evaluate alternative ways of raising tax revenue, of transportating coal from Newcastle to London, of abating air pollution, and so on.

Since the concern of economic analysis from the time of Adam Smith has been with the question of optimal resource utilization, the earliest welfare criteria date from classical welfare economics. Then, at the beginning of this century, Vilfredo Pareto developed what has come to be known as the New Welfare Economics. Since then additional welfare criteria have been suggested.

The Classical View of Social Welfare

The classical economists held a somewhat organic view of society, based on the notion that social welfare is greatest when all the individuals in society, as a group, are happiest. The satisfaction each individual gains from consuming goods and services is a psychic entity that the utilitarian philosophers called **utility.** Utility was viewed as a measurable amount of the psychic gratification received from consuming goods and services. Conceptually, a utility meter could be devised and strapped to the head of a consumer to register the intensity with which he or she enjoys certain goods and services. It was assumed that utility could be compared between individuals and between different types of goods. The utility I gain from watching a movie could be compared to that you enjoy when eating an orange.

Since social welfare is maximized when the sum total of the utilities for all individuals is the greatest, it would appear that the greatest social welfare would result from distributing goods in accordance with individuals' hedonistic capacities. Those with the greatest capacity for pleasure would receive the lion's share of the national product. However, the classical view was considerably more egalitarian. It assumed that all individuals have the same capacity for enjoying goods and services. But, for any individual, as more goods are consumed, the additional utility associated with consuming even more diminishes. Thus at high income levels gains in income will add less to utility than at low income levels.

The assumption that all individuals have the same capacity for enjoying goods and services, coupled with the proposition that gains in income produce less utility at high income levels than at low levels of income, led classical welfare economists to conclude that the distribution of income that would maximize social welfare is perfect equality. Suppose the individuals in an economy had the identical consumption utility functions shown in Table 2–1. **Marginal utility** (MU) is the increment to total utility associated with an additional $1,000 consumption of goods and services. As consumption increases, marginal utility declines. Suppose the economy consists of three families who consume all their income. GNP is $6,000. Table 2–2 shows three alternative distributions of income. In case I one family receives all the income and total utility is 350. As

TABLE 2–1
Utility as a Function of Total Consumption

Consumption (Dollars)	Utility	Marginal Utility
0	0	
1,000	100	100
2,000	180	80
3,000	240	60
4,000	285	45
5,000	320	35
6,000	350	30

income is distributed more uniformly between the three families, total utility rises. In case III, where income distribution is exactly equal, utility is 540, representing the maximum total utility.

This result can be derived in another way. Suppose we consider transferring $1,000 from family 1 to family 2. The gain in utility is the marginal utility of consumption for family 2, MU_2. The loss is the marginal utility of consumption for family 1, MU_1. If family 1 is at a higher consumption level than family 2 and if marginal utility is a decreasing function of consumption, then

$$\text{Gain} = MU_2 > MU_1 = \text{loss}$$

that is, the gain exceeds the loss. Given identical individual consumption utility functions and diminishing marginal utility, whenever the distribution of consumption is unequal a redistribution toward greater equality will always result in gains exceeding losses and an improvement in social welfare. Assuming that all income is either consumed now or saved for consumption at some future date, this implies that income equality is a desirable social goal.

TABLE 2–2
Total Utility Associated with Alternative
Distributions of Income

Case I:

Family	Income (Dollars)	Utility
1	6,000	350
2	0	0
3	0	0
Total	6,000	350

Case II:

Family	Income (Dollars)	Utility
1	3,000	240
2	2,000	180
3	1,000	100
Total	6,000	520

Case III:

Family	Income (Dollars)	Utility
1	2,000	180
2	2,000	180
3	2,000	180
Total	6,000	540

The Pareto Optimum

Some economists of the neoclassical school were skeptical of the utility approach. The classical welfare criterion depended on the interpersonal comparability of the psychic gratification individuals receive from consuming goods. Yet not only is utility impossible to measure, so that the assumption that individuals have identical consumption utility functions cannot be empirically verified, but the latter proposition did not seem reasonable, even on an a priori basis. Thus the neoclassical economists felt that the utility concept was a weak reed upon which to rest welfare statements about resource allocation.

Vilfredo Pareto developed a welfare criterion that requires no comparison of individual utilities: A **Pareto optimum** *is a situation in which no one can be made better off without making someone else worse off.* Stated somewhat differently, if some people prefer a change and no one objects, then the change must be an improvement over the present state of affairs.

As we shall see, the Pareto criterion does not require the use of the utility concept. However, its usefulness is limited, since there are many alternatives that cannot be ranked by this criterion. Consider the familiar case of a highway authority attempting to construct a long-needed road between two growing towns. A single family refuses to sell its property, which is located directly in the path of the planned highway. The property is assessed at $25,000, and the family agrees this is a fair market value. Rerouting the highway would cost the government an estimated $500,000. The government offers the family $50,000 for the property and still it refuses to sell.

Can welfare economics provide criteria by which to judge the desirability of a court-ordered sale of the property to the government? The Pareto criterion implies that a change will not necessarily be an improvement if it harms someone. Clearly, since the family finds the change undesirable, it cannot be ranked an improvement by the Pareto criterion. On the other hand, classical welfare theory would suggest that the change would be an improvement, since it will make many people better off and only a few worse off. However, such a judgment requires comparison of the utility of the many associated with the use of the new road and the loss of utility (disutility) to the few associated with the loss of their home. The new welfare economics does not make such comparisons.

It is important not to be misled by the term *Pareto optimum,* since a Pareto optimum is not a unique allocation of resources. There are many different Pareto optimal resource allocations consistent with different distributions of utility among the individuals of a society. Suppose the government has $1 million to spend on poverty areas in the United States. One possibility is to concentrate the spending in a single area, the Appalachian region, for instance, in the hopes of making a significant impact on growth. Another is to distribute the funds uniformly among the designated poverty areas of the country. In the latter case, the impact on any one region will be less but more areas will be affected. Presumably, either program could be designed to be Pareto optimal, that is, no resources would be wasted and no further improvements could be made without making someone worse off. Yet the distributive impact of the two programs would be quite different. Furthermore, changing from one to the other, once one is established, would not meet the Pareto criterion for an improvement, since the gain to some region(s) would be at the expense of others.[2]

Movement to a Pareto optimal resource allocation from one that is not Pareto optimal is not necessarily an improvement if a change in income distribution is involved. Suppose the Appalachian program is designed by efficiency experts with a view to eliminating all conceivable areas of waste. The alternative scheme of uniform distribution of funds is to be planned and administered locally, with a likelihood of considerable waste and inefficiency. Assuming the first program is Pareto optimal and the second is not, it would not be an improvement by the Pareto criterion to move from the second (nonoptimal program) to the first (optimal program), since some regions will lose as the Appalachian program gains. On the other hand, the Pareto criterion can be used to examine the way resources are being allocated in the second program. If the situation is nonoptimal, a better, Pareto optimal allocation can be found. Elimination of waste and inefficient techniques in the second program could make some people better off without hurting others, given the decision to distribute poverty funds on a uniform regional basis.

Contemporary Welfare Criteria

Recognizing the limitations of the Pareto criterion for ranking many alternatives, some contemporary economists have tried to develop more restrictive welfare criteria. In the spirit of the Paretian welfare economics, these criteria seek to avoid the use of the utility concept.[3]

One example of such formulation follows. Suppose, in the earlier example, the highway authority finally induces the family to sell its property by offering $100,000. Even though the family is unhappy with the move, the offer of $100,-000 allows them to compensate for their loss by purchasing other goods and services. The government is better off, since it saves $400,000 of the cost of relocating the road. If the family accepts the payment voluntarily, then clearly the family prefers that option and the situation can be ranked as an improvement by the Pareto criterion. If, on the other hand, it is coerced into the arrangement, the family experiences a loss in utility and consequently interpersonal utility comparison must be made to rank the change an improvement.

---

[2] The term *Pareto optimum* is an unfortunate choice. We will apply the term *Pareto efficiency* to an allocation that satisfies the Pareto criterion.

[3] Attempts at developing such criteria include J. R. Hicks, "The Foundations of Welfare Economics," *Economic Journal*, LXIX (December 1939), pp. 696–712; Nicholas Kaldor, "Welfare Propositions in Economics and Interpersonal Comparisons of Utility," *Economic Journal*, LXIX (September 1939), pp. 549–552; and Tibor Scitovsky, "A Note on Welfare Propositions in Economics," *Review of Economic Studies*, IX (1941–42), pp. 77–78.

Another type of criterion explicitly introduces value judgments concerning the desirability of alternative utility (or income) distributions.[4] It might suggest that the family be forced to sell its property for $25,000 on the grounds that the social need for the highway is more urgent than the interest of the individual family. Such a criterion, however, is subjective and requires some mechanism for making the value judgment. A different arbiter might decide that the maintenance of individual freedom is worth more than the $500,000 required to reroute the road.

Several procedures have been suggested for making such value judgments, including various voting arrangements. However, a voting arrangement also requires value judgments about how votes should be distributed. For instance, if everyone gets one vote, does this violate the utility principle if income-utility relations are different for different individuals?

We will consider these contemporary welfare criteria in more detail in the final chapter of this book. In the rest of this chapter we will explore the implications of the Pareto criterion in more detail.

2-3   CONDITIONS FOR PARETO OPTIMALITY

The Pareto criterion, that a change is an improvement if someone is made better off without making anyone worse off, can be used to derive certain conditions to determine if the criterion is satisfied in a particular case. When the Pareto criterion is satisfied, resource allocation is said to be efficient.[5] Consequently, these conditions are sometimes called **efficiency conditions.**

Efficiency in Production

Pareto efficiency implies that when a certain quantity of resources is devoted to the production of a single commodity, it is always best to produce as much as possible. More is always preferred to less when no additional resources are required to produce it and when the production of other goods and services is not affected.

Consider two firms producing a single commodity, bearings. For each firm, a production function is shown in Table 2-3. A **production function** is a relation between factor input and product output. In this case, labor is the only input in the production process.[6] Technologically, firm B is clearly the more efficient producer of bearings. For any given quantity of labor input, firm B produces

---

[4] For an example of this type of analysis see Paul A. Samuelson, "Social Indifference Curves," *Quarterly Journal of Economics,* LXX (February 1956), pp. 1-22.

[5] Paretian efficiency, also called allocative efficiency, should not be confused with technological efficiency, which refers to the least cost use of inputs in a production process. While allocative efficiency implies the achievement of technological efficiency, the converse is not the case.

[6] Other inputs may be used, but we have assumed they are present in fixed amounts.

TABLE 2–3
Production of Bearings as a Function of Labor Input

	FIRM A	
Labor Input (100 Man-Hours)	Output (1,000 Units)	Marginal Product (MP_{LA})
0	0	
1	50	50
2	90	40
3	120	30
4	145	25
5	165	20
	FIRM B	
Labor Input (100 Man-Hours)	Output (1,000 Units)	Marginal Product (MP_{LB})
0	0	
1	100	100
2	175	75
3	225	50
4	255	30
5	275	20

more bearings than firm A.[7] Suppose the available supply of labor is 400 man-hours. What is the best way to allocate labor between these firms?

At first glance, it may appear that since firm B is more efficient, all the labor should be used in firm B to produce 255,000 bearings. But suppose we consider reallocating 100 man-hours to firm A. Output in firm B will fall to 225,000 and output in firm A will be 50,000. Total output rises from 255,000 to 275,000.

How do we know when a reallocation results in an improvement? One way to look at the problem is to examine the gains and losses associated with a change. The change in output associated with a stipulated change in labor input is called the **marginal product of labor** (MP_L).

In Table 2–3 marginal product is given per 100 man-hours of labor input. The gains and losses associated with a reallocation of 100 man-hours of labor between firms is measured by the marginal product. Thus, in this case, since the marginal product of labor in firm A is greater than in firm B, the gain associated with moving 100 man-hours of labor from firm B to firm A exceeds the loss, that is,

$$\text{Gain} = MP_{LA} = 50 > 30 = MP_{LB} = \text{loss}$$

---

[7] Superior technological efficiency may be due to superior management or more modern capital equipment. We will deal with the determinants of production relations in chapter 6.

where MP_{LA} is the marginal product of labor in A and MP_{LB} is the marginal product of labor in B.

Unless the marginal product of labor is equal in both firms, there will be some reallocation of labor for which the gain will exceed the loss or for which the loss will exceed the gain. Thus labor should be allocated between the two firms until the gain in output in the firm receiving labor is exactly equal to the loss in output in the other firm. This implies that the marginal product of labor be equal in the two firms, that is,

$$MP_{LA} = MP_{LB}$$

More generally, the marginal product of a factor input must be equal in all firms producing the same product.

If 400 man-hours are available, the most efficient allocation of resources is 300 man-hours to firm B and 100 man-hours to firm A. At this point, both would be producing where $MP_L = 50$, that is,

$$MP_{LA} = MP_{LB} = 50$$

Suppose there is a central planning board (CPB) responsible for ensuring efficient resource allocation in this economy. How could the CPB induce firms to hire the efficient amount of labor? It could set the price of labor at its marginal product. That is, each firm would be required to pay to the CPB the value of 50,000 bearings for each 100 man-hours it uses. Firm A would break even hiring 100 man-hours of labor. Firm B would hire exactly 300 man-hours. More workers would add less to output than their wage, so hiring them would incur a loss, while fewer workers would generate excess profits, and hence an increment would represent a gain. Thus the CPB could use a pricing scheme to achieve efficient resource allocation.

Suppose labor supply in the bearing industry rises to 700 man-hours. Now 100 additional man-hours should go to firm B and 200 additional man-hours to firm A, equalizing MP_L at 30. If the CPB sets the price of labor at the value of 30,000 bearings per 100 man-hours of labor and firms maximize their net gains, or profits, this allocation will be achieved.

Diminishing Returns and Efficiency

The production functions in Table 2–3 both display constantly diminishing marginal labor productivity. There are a number of reasons why we expect this **principle of diminishing returns** to apply in production. If other factor inputs are fixed, it is likely that the rate of increase of total product will slow down as more labor is applied unless the other factor inputs are also increased. It is much easier to study alone, for instance, than in a crowded library. Agricultural output increases more rapidly if fertilizer is added to newly seeded land.

Diminishing marginal productivity ensures that the efficiency condition

$$MP_{LA} = MP_{LB}$$

will result in a maximum rather than a minimum level of output. If marginal product were increasing, it would often be better to assign all labor to a single firm.[8] However, for reasons that we will consider in chapter 6, diminishing marginal productivity is likely to apply in most cases.

Alternative Production Techniques

In the previous example we were interested in maximizing the level of output from a single, limited resource. We may also be interested in the optimal utilization of *alternative* resources at each level of output. A firm generally has a number of different ways in which various resources can be combined to produce a certain level of output.

Table 2–4 shows alternative production technologies for two firms producing bearings. Suppose the total amount of capital available is 120 and the amount of labor, 180. Firm A, which is relatively more efficient in capital-intensive methods, is producing 100,000 bearings by its most capital-intensive process, using 100 capital and 20 labor. Firm B, which is relatively more efficient in labor-intensive methods, uses 20 capital and 160 labor (its most labor-intensive process) to produce 100,000 bearings. Now suppose we consider a reallocation of resources between the two firms.

Suppose firm B were to release 60 units of labor to firm A. In order to maintain production at the 100,000 level, B would require 20 units of capital. On the other hand, if A acquires 60 labor from B, it could release 60 capital and maintain production. Thus 40 units of capital are freed for use in some other productive activity. Clearly, since production can be maintained using fewer resources, the change represents an improvement. Now suppose firm B considers a move to a more capital-intensive process. Moving from B_4 to B_3 releases 40 labor and requires 20 additional capital. If the 40 released labor were used in firm A, 20 capital would be released. In other words, production will be exactly maintained at previous levels and there is no gain from a reallocation. If firm B were to move to a still more capital-intensive process, it would release 1 unit of labor for every 3 units of capital it requires. On the other hand, firm A would require 5 units of labor for every 4 units of capital released to B to maintain bearing production at the 100,000 level. Consequently, the move would result in a decline in production and would represent an inferior reallocation.

The rate at which one resource is released when another is added to produce a

---

[8] This firm need not be the firm with increasing *MP*, however. Consider the following:

	FIRM C			FIRM D	
Input	Output	MP	Input	Output	MP
1	100	100	1	25	25
2	175	75	2	75	50 ˙
3	230	55	3	130	55

If 3,000 man-hours are available, they should all be allocated to firm C for maximum efficiency, even though firm D experiences increasing marginal labor productivity.

TABLE 2–4
Alternative Resource Combinations Required
to Produce 100,000 Bearings

		FIRM A	
	Capital (K_A)	Labor (L_A)	Marginal Rate of Substitution (MRS)
1.	100	20	
			$1/2$
2.	80	30	
			$5/4$
3.	40	80	
			2
4.	20	120	
			8
5.	10	200	

		FIRM B	
	Capital (K_B)	Labor (L_B)	Marginal Rate of Substitution (MRS)
1.	200	20	
			$1/4$
2.	120	40	
			$1/3$
3.	60	60	
			2
4.	40	100	
			3
5.	20	160	

fixed level of output is called the **marginal rate of factor substitution** (MRS). Suppose the marginal rate of substitution of labor for capital in firm B is greater than that for firm A, that is,

$$MRS_{LK}^B > MRS_{LK}^A$$

If B moves to a more capital-intensive process, more labor is released from B than is required by A to maintain production at the reduced level of capital. If B moves to a more labor-intensive process, it will require more labor than can be released from A if A is to maintain production. Only in the case where the marginal rate of factor substitution is equal for the two firms, that is,

$$MRS_{LK}^B = MRS_{LK}^A$$

will the amount of one factor released from one firm be the exact amount required to maintain production in the other. Consequently, no reallocation of factors would represent an improvement. Equal marginal rates of factor substitution for all firms producing the same product is the second Pareto efficiency criterion.

Notice that to derive this result we assumed that the MRS_{LK} is constantly increasing as processes become more labor-intensive. This implies that the more labor is being used relative to capital the more labor can be released as new capital is acquired without affecting the level of output. It is consistent with the principle of diminishing returns that the more abundant one factor is relative to another the less will one more unit add to total output. The more fertilizer we have applied to an acre of land the smaller will be the impact on output of an additional application.

How could the central planning board ensure that all firms will produce at equal marginal rates of factor substitution? In this case, the CPB could announce that all firms producing bearings may acquire all the capital and labor resources they wish but that the price of capital is twice that of labor. Firms would acquire resources until no further gains or losses are realized. This would occur where the acquisition of an additional unit of capital is equivalent to a loss of two units of labor. By setting the price of capital at twice that of labor, the CPB can induce firms to adopt the production technology for which a unit of capital is worth two units of labor. The second efficiency criterion,

$$MRS_{LK}^B = MRS_{LK}^A$$

established that this is the optimal production plan for the firms in this problem.

Alternative Production Possibilities

Suppose we consider firms that are producing more than one good: Two firms are producing bearings and screws, using a single resource, labor. Table 2–5 shows the alternative output combinations that each firm can produce per man-hour of labor input.

Imagine that firm A is producing 40 bearings and 45 screws per man-hour and firm B is producing 30 bearings and 27 screws per man-hour, and that we desire a reallocation of resources to increase screw production. In firm A, when the production of screws is increased by 10, bearing output falls by 20. For this firm, the cost of producing 10 additional screws is the forgone revenue from the sale of 20 bearings. Put in another way, the cost of screws in terms of bearings is 2. When 10 additional screws are produced in firm B, bearing output falls by only 10. In B the bearing cost per screw is 1. Given the initial levels of output, firm B is the low cost producer of screws, cost being measured in terms of foregone bearing production. The bearing cost of screws is called the **marginal rate of transformation** (MRT). Clearly, if an increase in screw output is desired, the increase should come from the firm with the lowest MRT.

Suppose no increase in screw production is desired. Is there any reallocation

TABLE 2–5
Alternative Combinations of Bearings and Screws that
Can Be Produced Per Man-Hour of Labor

	FIRM A	
		Marginal Rate of Transformation $\left(-\dfrac{\Delta B}{\Delta S}\right)$
Bearings	Screws	
100	0	
		1
80	20	
		$1\frac{1}{3}$
60	35	
		2
40	45	
		4
20	50	
		10
0	52	

	FIRM B	
		Marginal Rate of Transformation $\left(-\dfrac{\Delta B}{\Delta S}\right)$
Bearings	Screws	
50	0	
		$\frac{2}{3}$
40	15	
		$\frac{5}{6}$
30	27	
		1
20	37	
		$1\frac{1}{4}$
10	45	
		$2\frac{1}{4}$
0	51	

of resources within firms that could increase the output of screws using no additional resources? Firm B can produce screws at a lower bearing cost than A. On the other hand, the screw cost of bearings is lower for A. If B were to produce 10 more screws and A 10 fewer screws, bearing output would fall by 10 in B and rise by 20 in A. This would result in a net increase of 10 bearings with no decline in screw production. Although each firm must give up screws to produce additional bearings, a reallocation of resources among several firms can increase bearing output with no sacrifice of screws. This will be the case as long as *MRT*, that is, the bearing price of screws, is unequal among the firms.

Suppose that the bearing cost of screws is greater in firm A than in firm B, that is,

$$MRT_A = \left(-\frac{\Delta B}{\Delta S}\right)_A > \left(-\frac{\Delta B}{\Delta S}\right)_B = MRT_B$$

where ΔB refers to a change in bearing production and ΔS refers to a change in screw production. If resources are reallocated so that net screw production is left unchanged, that is,

$$-\Delta S_A = \Delta S_B$$

then bearing production in firm A will increase by more than it decreases in B, that is,

$$\Delta B_A > -\Delta B_B$$

As long as *MRT* is different among firms, a reallocation of resources within firms will always result in an improvement. Thus the third efficiency condition can be restated

$$MRT_A = MRT_B$$

Another way to state this criterion is that the opportunity cost of one good in terms of another must be the same for all firms producing the goods. Opportunity cost refers to the output of a good forgone when another is produced.

The statement that all firms should be producing at equal *MRT* is another form of the well-known **principle of comparative advantage** in international trade. Notice that firm B is a relatively inefficient producer of both screws and bearings, that is, output per man-hour is lower than in firm A. Yet in terms of bearings, B can produce screws cheaper than A. If A and B were two countries trading, it would pay B to produce more screws and obtain its bearings from A. B could obtain bearings from A at a price of one-half screw per bearing,[9] while it would cost one screw per bearing to produce bearings domestically.

If certain resources or resource combinations were better suited to bearing than to screw production, it is likely that the bearing cost of screws would rise as more screws are produced. If *MRT* rose in both firms (or countries), it is probable that the optimal degree of specialization would require both to produce some of each commodity, although one firm (or country) might produce relatively more of one commodity than the other. On the other hand, if *MRT* were constant for both firms or countries (as is the case in most examples from international trade textbooks), then optimal specialization would entail complete specialization

---

[9] The actual price of bearings will lie between one-half screw and one screw, depending upon the elasticity of reciprocal demand for screws and bearings in the two countries.

in the production of that commodity for which MRT is lowest. Notice that equality of MRTs will only occur when MRT is not constant, and the criterion results in an optimum only when MRT rises as more of a good is being produced. If the opportunity cost of producing bearings were to fall the more bearings were produced, then complete specialization would be the most desirable way to organize production. As we will see in chapter 6, this is unlikely to be the case.

If the central planning board were to establish a fixed bearing price for screws, then firms would reorganize production until

$$MRT = p_S$$

where p_S is the bearing price of screws. If MRT were less than p_S, firms would increase screw output, since the addition to revenue, p_S, would be greater than the addition to cost, MRT. On the other hand, firms would cut back screw production if the bearing cost (MRT) exceeded the price. Since MRT rises and falls with screw production, adjustments would continue until MRT equaled p_S. If all firms could sell screws at p_S, all firms would be producing at equal marginal rates of transformation. Thus, the CPB could establish efficiency in production.

Efficiency in Consumption

The Pareto criterion states that a change will be an improvement if someone can be made better off without making someone else worse off. In order to establish welfare changes associated with production alternatives, we must consider how such changes are evaluated by households.

Consider two neighbors, Tom and Jerry, who are do-it-yourself repairmen, maintaining home inventories of hardware, including screws and bearings. Tom proposes a trade of screws for bearings. He is willing to trade 3 bearings for 1 screw. Jerry, on the other hand, would be willing to accept 2 bearings for 1 screw. Suppose Tom acquires 10 screws from Jerry for 30 bearings. Tom is no worse off, or he would not have made the trade. On the other hand, Jerry is better off, since he would have made the trade for 20 bearings and he actually received 30, a bonus of 10.

The terms on which an individual is willing to trade one good for another is called the **marginal rate of product substitution** (MRS). Clearly, at least one party will benefit from a trade if the MRS's of the two individuals differ. If I am twice as fond of apples as of oranges and you like apples and oranges equally well, then, if we both have apples and oranges, we could both gain from a trade. You will be better off if I give you more than one orange per apple, and I will be better off giving you anything less than two oranges per apple. The terms on which the trade is actually made will fall somewhere between the different marginal rates of product substitution. If these rates are the same, then the exchange would be made at MRS, which would leave everyone exactly as well off as before the trade. Equality of the marginal rate of product substitution between any two goods for all individuals in the economy, that is,

$$MRS^I = MRS^{II}$$

is the fourth Pareto criterion. It implies that no further trade or reallocation can be made to make someone better off without making someone else worse off.

In this example, the terms of trade for bearings and screws were established by the trading partners. Suppose a bearing price for screws were set by the central planning board. Persons whose marginal rates of substitution were greater than the set price would buy screws and those with lower MRS would sell them. Clearly MRS, that is, the relative preference for screws over bearings, will decrease the more screws and the fewer bearings an individual possesses. As households with high MRS acquire more screws and those with low MRS more bearings, their relative preferences at the margin move to equality. Although the consumption pattern of some households may be relatively "screw-intensive" and that of others more "bearing-intensive," at the margin (for the final trade) each household's MRS will exactly equal the terms of trade for all households that consume some of both goods. Thus the CPB, by offering to buy and sell screws at a fixed bearing price, can ensure efficiency in consumption.

Global Efficiency

So far we have defined the conditions for Pareto optimal resource utilization in production and for Pareto optimal distribution in consumption.[10] We still must determine that what is produced satisfies the requirements of consumers.

Recall that the marginal rate of transformation between two goods (which must be equal for all firms producing both goods if efficiency is to be achieved) tells us how much of one we must give up to obtain one more unit of the other. On the other hand, the marginal rate of product substitution (which must be equal for all households consuming both goods if efficiency is to be achieved) tells us how much of one good the household is willing to forgo in order to obtain the other without feeling worse off.

The fifth Pareto criterion states that the optimal scale of production of the two goods from the point of view of the consuming sector occurs where the marginal rate of product substitution equals the marginal rate of transformation, that is,

$$MRS = MRT$$

To see why this must be so, consider the possibility that the marginal rate of substitution is greater than the marginal rate of transformation, that is,

$$-\frac{\Delta B^H}{\Delta S^H} = MRS > MRT = -\frac{\Delta B^F}{\Delta S^F}$$

This implies that households are willing to give up more of one good for the other than is necessary given the production alternatives. Consequently, they would

---

[10] Note that Pareto optimal distribution in consumption can be defined for any distribution of income. This refers only to the distribution of particular goods and services among individuals given the distribution of purchasing power, or income.

gain if more resources were allocated to produce that good, say bearings. As bearings production rises, so does MRT, while MRS falls as households acquire more bearings. On the other hand, if

$$MRS < MRT$$

the cost of producing more bearings is greater than households are willing to pay. Fewer bearings (and more screws) should be produced until the marginal rates of substitution and transformation are brought into equality.[11]

Another way to look at the question of global efficiency is to evaluate the gains and losses associated with a reallocation. Suppose MRS of bearings for screws is 3, while MRT is 2, that is,

$$-\frac{\Delta B^H}{\Delta S^H} = MRS = 3 > 2 = MRT = -\frac{\Delta B^F}{\Delta S^F}$$

Households are willing to give up 3 bearings to obtain 1 screw. This means the welfare value of the screw is 3 bearings. The cost of producing a screw is 2 bearings. Thus, if resources are reallocated from bearing to screw production, the gain (bearing value) is 3, while the loss is 2. The gain, or MRS, exceeds the loss, or MRT, and so the change will be an improvement.

Global Efficiency and Absolute Levels of Production

Suppose the central planning board agrees to buy and sell screws at a fixed price, p_S. Producers will be induced to reallocate resources within firms until

$$MRT = p_S$$

Households will buy and sell screws for bearings until

$$MRS = p_S$$

As long as the CPB sets the same price for both firms and households, and the former argument applies where the reallocation is to more screws and fewer bearings, this will ensure that

$$MRS = p_S = MRT$$

and the condition for global efficiency would appear to be satisfied.

However, the establishment of fixed prices at which commodities can be

---

[11] Note that if

$$-\frac{\Delta B^H}{\Delta S^H} = MRS_{BS} < MRT_{BS} = -\frac{\Delta B^F}{\Delta S^F}$$

where MRS_{BS} is the marginal rate of substitution of bearings for screws, then

$$-\frac{\Delta S^H}{\Delta B^H} = MRS_{SB} > MRT_{SB} = -\frac{\Delta S^F}{\Delta B^F}$$

where MRS_{SB} is the marginal rate of substitution of screws for bearings.

bought and sold only ensures that at the margin, *changes* in screw and bearing output will be matched by *changes* in consumer purchases, that is,

$$-\frac{\Delta B^H}{\Delta S^H} = MRS = p_S = MRT = -\frac{\Delta B^F}{\Delta S^F}$$

It does not ensure that the actual *level* of screw and bearing production will be equal to the total amount consumers wish to purchase at p_S, that is,

$$S^H = S^F \quad \text{and} \quad B^H = B^F$$

But global efficiency does require that the amount consumers wish to purchase at p_S be exactly equal to the amount produced at p_S. If consumers are not willing to purchase all the screws produced at p_S, then there will be an excess supply of screws, which is wasteful in the face of scarcity. Fewer resources should have been allocated to screws to begin with.

Suppose

$$MRS = 2.5 = MRT$$

and the CPB sets

$$p_S = 2.5$$

When *MRT* is 2.5, firms produce 20,000 bearings and 50,000 screws. *MRS* is 2.5 when consumers purchase 45,000 bearings and 40,000 screws. Thus, when p_S is 2.5, 20,000 bearings and 50,000 screws will be produced. But households will only purchase 40,000 screws, leaving an excess supply of 10,000. Furthermore, households will attempt to purchase 45,000 bearings when only 20,000 are available. Thus the establishment of fixed commodity prices by the CPB does not necessarily produce global efficiency. For global efficiency the condition

$$MRS = MRT$$

must be met, and *in addition,* the amount of each good produced must equal the amount consumers wish to purchase, that is,

$$S^H = S^F \quad \text{and} \quad B^H = B^F$$

We will return to this question in chapters 3 and 4.

Optimal Supply of Resources

The principle of equalizing marginal rates of product substitution among goods with their marginal rates of transformation for global efficiency can also be applied to the theory of optimal factor supply. Earlier we saw that although resources are scarce, they nevertheless may be used for other than productive purposes in ways that contribute to social welfare. An alternative to the use of labor is leisure. Resources devoted to the production of capital goods can be used for the more immediate production of consumer goods.

Consider the optimal amount of labor force participation. From a different perspective, this is equivalent to the optimal consumption of leisure. A household has a certain amount of the labor resource available. Conceivably both husband and wife could work twenty-four hours each. However, with maximum work effort the welfare value of leisure would be nearly infinite, since such efforts would result in rapid physical deterioration. Given the number of available hours, the household must decide whether to allocate them to labor force participation, for which it receives income, or to leisure, which provides welfare value. Since income can be used to purchase goods, both income and leisure provide welfare value. The marginal rate of substitution of income for leisure is the rate at which a household is willing to sacrifice income for leisure. For instance, a family may be willing to forgo $3 of income for an additional hour of leisure. Furthermore, MRS of income for leisure (MRS_{Yl}) is likely to increase the more hours are devoted to work and the fewer to leisure.

Our Pareto criterion suggests that optimal consumption of leisure occurs where the marginal rate of substitution of income for leisure equals the opportunity cost of leisure in terms of income, that is,

$$MRS_{Yl} = MRT_{Yl}$$

The marginal rate of transformation of income for leisure is the amount of income (in the form of goods and services) forgone when one man-hour is withheld from the labor force. From the viewpoint of the whole economy the amount of goods and services forgone when labor is reduced is the marginal product of labor, MP_L. Thus the efficiency condition for optimal labor supply can be expressed as

$$MRS_{Yl} = MP_L$$

Furthermore, the demand for labor must equal the supply when the marginal condition is met.

Suppose the central planning board sets a fixed wage at which firms hire labor. From the viewpoint of the households the wage represents the price they must pay to consume leisure. They will consume leisure until the welfare value of the last hour, MRS_{Yl}, exactly equals its price, that is, until

$$MRS_{Yl} = w$$

Firms will hire labor until the opportunity value of the last worker hired in terms of output, MP_L, equals the wage, that is, until

$$MP_L = w$$

Thus the establishment of a fixed wage ensures that the marginal condition for the optimal degree of labor force participation is met, since the condition

$$MRS_{Yl} = w = MP_L$$

is satisfied. However, setting a fixed wage does not ensure that the demand for labor will equal the supply. There may be involuntary unemployment of labor (excess supply) even though the marginal condition for global efficiency is satisfied.

Allocation of Resources to Investment

A similar analysis can be made for the efficient allocation of resources to producing capital equipment. Capital may consist of physical plant and machines that are used to produce other goods and services. Another way to devote resources to indirect production of goods is by training labor to perform more productively. Investment of current labor resources for making labor more productive is called investment in **human capital.** One way to explain why different people earn different rates of pay is that they have acquired different amounts of human capital. Thus part of their income is not a pure wage but is a return on human capital.

Suppose a household wishes to invest part of its available labor-leisure time in the acquisition of human capital. The household may want to decide whether the mother should go to college or whether she should go to work as a secretary. Assuming that she is indifferent to the way in which she uses her time (that is, she has no preference for secretarial work per se over studying), the monetary gain to the family of investment in human capital (education) is the difference in income she could expect as a college graduate over her secretarial pay. However, to obtain the increase in income the family must wait several years. Most people have a subjective preference for current consumption over future consumption. The rate at which a household is willing to exchange future consumption for current consumption is called the marginal rate of substitution of future for present consumption, MRS_{fp}. The MRS_{fp} is generally greater than 1, that is, a household will give up \$1 of consumption today only if it can expect to receive more than \$1 tomorrow.[12] Thus

$$MRS_{fp} = 1 + \tau$$

where τ is the extra amount of future consumption required to compensate the household for giving up current consumption.

The Pareto criterion suggests that the efficient level of capital accumulation occurs where the marginal rate of substitution of future for present consumption equals the marginal rate of transformation, that is,

$$MRS_{fp} = MRT_{fp}$$

The rate at which future consumption can be transformed into present consumption, MRT_{fp}, is $1 + \rho$, where ρ is the rate of return on capital. For human capital, this is the per cent increase in expected income as a result of training.

---

[12] This helps to explain why borrowers must pay interest to lenders.

For physical capital, this is sometimes called the marginal productivity of capital, MP_K.[13] Thus efficiency occurs where

$$MRS_{fp} = 1 + \tau = 1 + \rho = MRT_{fp}$$

The family should invest in a college education for the mother as long as the rate at which it is willing to exchange future for present consumption is greater than the expected increase in her income after graduation. Alternatively, investment should take place where

$$\tau = \rho$$

For global efficiency in the allocation of resources to capital goods, not only must the marginal condition be met but the amount of resources households wish to release from current consumption must be equal to the amount firms wish to invest. The central planning board could influence firms' and households' decisions to use current resources for capital accumulation by setting a fixed rate of interest i. The quantity $1 + i$ represents the opportunity cost to households of current spending. Thus households will borrow or lend until the subjective rate at which they would exchange the last dollar of future consumption for present consumption is equal to the opportunity cost of present consumption, that is,

$$1 + \tau = MRS_{fp} = 1 + i$$

or

$$\tau = i$$

The quantity $1 + i$ is also the opportunity cost for firms investing current resources, since these same resources could be sold and the proceeds loaned at interest. Thus capital accumulation will take place until the return from the last unit is equal to the interest rate, that is,

$$\rho = i$$

or

$$1 + \rho = MRT_{fp} = 1 + i$$

The establishment of a fixed rate of interest by the CPB thus ensures that the marginal condition for the efficient rate of capital accumulation is met, since the condition

$$MRS_{fp} = 1 + i = MRT_{fp}$$

is satisfied. However, setting a fixed rate of interest does not ensure that the supply of resources from current consumption will be equal to the demand at that interest rate. Some mechanism other than a pricing arrangement must be introduced to ensure that supply equals demand in product and factor markets.

---

[13] Alternatively, the compound rate of return on capital investment is sometimes called the internal rate of return or the marginal efficiency of capital.

2-4 THE MARGINAL CONDITIONS AND ECONOMIC EFFICIENCY

It is important to keep in mind that the so-called marginal conditions for economic efficiency are derived from the Pareto criterion:

A change is an improvement if someone is made better off without making anyone else worse off.

The marginal conditions are merely rules of thumb for achieving the Pareto optimum. They are only valid as rules of thumb if certain assumptions are met. For instance, if opportunity costs do not increase as the output of a good increases, the condition that all firms producing the good operate at the same marginal rate of transformation produces a minimum rather than maximum level of output. Furthermore, if all costs of production are not accounted for in calculating the firm's marginal rate of transformation, then the marginal condition will not produce optimal results. This may occur if the smoke from a factory inflicts a real or psychic cost on nearby residents but is not included in calculating the production cost of the good by the firm managers.

Thus, while the Pareto criterion remains valid for making certain types of welfare comparisons,[14] the marginal conditions only reflect Pareto optimality under certain circumstances. Since the requisite assumptions are satisfied in many cases, economists often treat the marginal conditions as welfare criteria in themselves. However, it must be kept in mind that the attainment of the marginal conditions is only a means (in some cases) of fulfilling a larger objective, not an end in itself. In chapter 3 we will consider cases in which attainment of the marginal conditions does not imply efficient resource allocation.

QUESTIONS FOR STUDY AND REVIEW

1. Two firms use labor to produce widgets. Their production functions are as follows:

FIRM A		FIRM B	
Labor Input	Widgets	Labor Input	Widgets
1	500	1	300
2	900	2	550
3	1,250	3	700
4	1,500	4	800
5	1,600	5	850
6	1,675	6	875

a) Which firm is the low cost producer?

b) If 6 units of labor are available, how should they be distributed between the firms to ensure efficient use of resources?

c) What price should the central planning board charge the firms for the use of labor?

d) If the labor supply increases to 9, what price should the central planning board

---

[14] Remember that a Pareto optimum may be associated with an undesirable distribution of income.

charge the firms for the use of labor to ensure efficient resource allocation in the widget industry?

e) Suppose technological change in the widget industry reduces by one half the labor input requirement for each level of production for both firms. How would your answers to the above questions be affected?

2. "American agriculture is the most efficient in the world." Assuming that this is true, would the United States ever import agricultural goods? Be sure to justify your answer.

3. If economics is concerned with finding ways to achieve maximum *total* satisfaction from its limited resources, why are economists so concerned with *marginal* relations?

4. The idea that economic efficiency should be the most important *economic* goal of any society has been defended and denied. Present your views on the controversy, with some discussion on both sides of the question.

5. The principle of comparative advantage is usually associated with the theory of international trade. Generalize the principle and show its relation to the theory of resource allocation.

6. "If efficient resource allocation is a goal of an economy, then prices must exist in that economy." Comment.

ADDITIONAL READING

Bator, Francis M. "The Simple Analytics of Welfare Maximization," *American Economic Review,* XLVII (March 1957), pp. 22–59.

Baumol, William J. *Economic Theory and Operations Analysis,* 3d ed. Englewood Cliffs, N.J.: Prentice-Hall, 1972, chapter 16.

Kohler, Heinz. *Welfare and Planning.* New York: Wiley, 1966, chapter 2.

3 Economic Efficiency in a Market System

An economic system is a set of institutions and relations to allocate resources. Thus an economic system must determine what is to be produced, how it is to be produced, and to whom the product is to be distributed. Such decisions may be explicit or implicit. A central planning board operating on the basis of certain explicit criteria may assign target output levels for all industries, stipulate the way in which productive factors are used by individual firms, and ration the final products to households. Since allocative decisions are explicit, it is possible to ascertain if the predetermined allocative criteria are satisfied.

Where allocative decisions are made implicitly, as they are in a market system, a theoretical model is needed to demonstrate that the resultant allocation of resources is optimal. This was the contribution of Adam Smith in *The Wealth of Nations*. Although in a market economy allocative decisions are not made explicitly by a central planning board, or by tradition as in the medieval society, Smith attempted to show that the invisible hand of the market would produce a socially desirable resource allocation.

The possibility of efficient resource allocation is not, however, exclusive to market systems as Adam Smith had implied. There are other ways to organize production and distribution that will produce optimal allocative decisions. Furthermore, a market system may fail in many ways to achieve Pareto optimality. In this chapter we examine a market model in terms of the efficiency criteria. In chapter 4 we will discuss alternative economic systems.

3–1 THE THEORETICAL JUSTIFICATION FOR MARKETS

Consider an economy in which all goods and services as well as factors of production are traded in markets. A market is a theoretical construct in which a single price for a good or service is established. Market participants are influenced by prices in making their sales and purchases. If the quantity offered for sale is more or less than that desired by buyers at the prevailing market price, buyers and sellers will readjust their bids and offer prices until an **equilibrium** price is established. At such an equilibrium the exact quantity offered for sale is purchased by buyers and there is no additional demand for the good. Consequently, there will be no further re-adjustments in price by either buyers or sellers.

In this section we examine the way in which market participants — households and firms — decide the amount of goods and factor services to buy and sell on the basis of market prices. In particular, we are interested in whether or not their market decisions are consistent with the efficiency conditions set forth in chapter 2.

Efficiency in Product Markets

The Household

Since market prices are fixed by the interaction of many buyers and sellers, a household views these prices as given data in its decisions concerning how much of each good to purchase and the amount of factor services to supply. The purchasing power of each household is small in relation to the total demand for products, so the decision of any one household to rearrange its purchases will have a negligible effect on market price.

Households will view market prices as the opportunity costs of goods in terms of each other. If apples cost 5 cents and bananas 10 cents the opportunity cost of apples in terms of bananas is 2, the ratio of their prices, that is,

$$-\frac{\Delta A}{\Delta B} = \frac{p_B}{p_A}$$

Households will allocate their budgets between apples and bananas where they are equally happy with 2 apples and 1 banana, or equivalently where

$$MRS_{AB} = -\frac{\Delta A}{\Delta B} = \frac{p_B}{p_A}$$

Thus, between any two goods, X and Y, households will adjust their purchases until the MRS_{YX} is equal to the ratio of the product prices.

Notice that since p_X and p_Y are set in the markets for X and Y, all household units face identical prices, so that

$$MRS_{YX}^{I} = \frac{p_X}{p_Y} = MRS_{YX}^{II}$$

All households will adjust their purchases of X and Y until their marginal rates of product substitution are equal, satisfying the marginal condition for efficiency in consumption. This does not imply that all households purchase the same quantities of X and Y, but at the margin each household is willing to exchange additional units at the same rate.

The Firm

A similar analysis can be made of the behavior of firms. Suppose there are many sellers in the market and the output of any single firm is so small in relation to total market supply that its decision to increase or decrease output will have a negligible effect on market price. Under these conditions firms view selling price as fixed, since it is established by the interaction of many buyers and sellers in the market.

Firms in a market economy are assumed to adjust output levels to maximize their profits. The maximum profit level is reached when the firm can no longer increase output without increasing costs above the selling price of the good. The increase in cost associated with the production of an additional unit of output is called **marginal cost.** Marginal cost is generally assumed to rise with increasing output because of diminishing returns to fixed plant and equipment as additional labor and materials are employed. Marginal cost also increases if factor prices rise when the demand for those factors increases. Thus the maximum profit output occurs where price equals marginal cost, that is,

$$p = MC$$

The ratio of the marginal costs of any two goods is their marginal rate of transformation, that is,

$$-\frac{\Delta Y}{\Delta X} = \frac{MC_X}{MC_Y} = MRT_{YX}$$

Suppose the marginal cost of X is twice the marginal cost of Y. If we are willing to give up a unit of X, we can produce two additional Y at the same cost. Since profit-maximizing firms produce where marginal cost equals the price established in the market, that is,

$$p_X = MC_X \quad \text{and} \quad p_Y = MC_Y$$

it follows that

$$\frac{MC_X}{MC_Y} = \frac{p_X}{p_Y} = MRT_{YX}$$

Since all firms can sell their output at these prices, this implies that

$$MRT_{YX}^A = \frac{p_X}{p_Y} = MRT_{YX}^B$$

That is, X and Y will be produced at the same marginal rate of transformation throughout the economy. Thus another efficiency condition is satisfied.

Global Efficiency in Product Markets

A market system ensures that the two criteria for global efficiency are met. First, the market mechanism, by which bid and offer prices are continually readjusted until quantity supplied equals quantity demanded, ensures that there will be no excess supply of, or demand for, goods and services when the market is in equilibrium.

Furthermore, the marginal condition is also satisfied. Since the condition

$$MRS_{YX} = \frac{p_X}{p_Y}$$

is met in the household sector and the condition

$$MRT_{YX} = \frac{p_X}{p_Y}$$

is met in the producing sector, then when buyers and sellers trade at the market prices, the condition

$$MRS_{YX} = \frac{p_X}{p_Y} = MRT_{YX}$$

is also met. The price mechanism will ensure that the rate at which consumers are willing to exchange commodities is equal to the relative costs of the last units produced.

In a market system, therefore, the marginal condition for global efficiency is satisfied, and in addition there is no excess demand for, or supply of, goods and services. Thus global efficiency is achieved.

Efficiency in Factor Markets

As long as buyers and sellers act independently and each is so small in relation to the total market that his own actions will not perceptibly alter market prices, each adjusts his behavior with established market prices as given data.

The Firm

Firms, maximizing profits, will hire factors of production as long as the addition to revenue exceeds the addition to cost. The addition to revenue when a factor is employed is its marginal product multiplied by the product price (the **marginal value product**). The cost of employing the factor is the factor price established in the market. Thus, assuming the marginal product decreases as more of the factor is employed (in accordance with the principle of diminishing returns), the profit-maximizing firm will employ more of the factor until the marginal value product equals the factor price, that is,

$$p \times MP_f = p_f$$

where p is the product price, MP_f is the marginal factor productivity, and p_f is the factor price.

Since the factor price is established in the market, all firms must pay the same price. For two firms, A and B, producing the same good,

$$p \times MP_{fA} = p_f = p \times MP_{fB}$$

This implies

$$MP_{fA} = MP_{fB}$$

that is, marginal factor productivity is the same for both firms.

If more than one factor is employed (L and K, for instance), then

$$\frac{MP_{LA}}{MP_{KA}} = \frac{p_L}{p_K} = \frac{MP_{LB}}{MP_{KB}}$$

The ratio of marginal factor productivities is equal to the marginal rate of factor substitution, the rate at which factors can be substituted in production without altering the level of output. Suppose the last unit of labor adds 10 units of output, while the last unit of capital adds 5 units. We could substitute 2 capital per unit of labor without affecting output, that is,

$$-\frac{\Delta K}{\Delta L} = MRS_{KL} = \frac{MP_L}{MP_K} = 2$$

Since all firms must purchase factors of production at the prices established in the factor markets, profit-maximizing firms producing the same product will operate at equal marginal rates of factor substitution, that is,

$$MRS_{KL}^A = \frac{p_L}{p_K} = MRS_{KL}^B$$

The Household

Households will consume leisure where the marginal rate of substitution between other goods and leisure is equal to the price of leisure in terms of other goods. Income, Y, can be viewed as generalized purchasing power for goods other than leisure. The price of leisure in terms of other goods is the amount of income forgone when more leisure is consumed, the wage. Thus, households will consume leisure where the marginal rate of substitution of income for leisure equals the wage established in the labor market, that is,

$$MRS_{Yl} = w$$

Since this condition holds for the demand for leisure, it also holds for its mirror image, the supply of labor. Since all households must accept the wage established in the labor market, they will all supply labor (consume leisure) at equal marginal rates of substitution of income for leisure, that is,

$$MRS_{Yl}^I = w = MRS_{Yl}^{II}$$

Global Efficiency in Factor Markets

Under the conditions described, the two criteria for global efficiency are met in factor markets as well as in product markets. The market mechanism ensures that factor prices will be continually readjusted until there is no excess supply of, or demand for, productive factors.

In addition, the marginal conditions are satisfied. Firms will hire labor until the marginal value product is equal to the wage, that is,

$$p \times MP_L = w$$

If all prices are expressed in dollars, then the marginal value product of labor is the dollar value of the change in output when the last worker is hired. Thus the marginal value product is the marginal dollar product, $MP_L(\$)$, that is,

$$p \times MP_L = MP_L(\$)$$

and

$$w = MP_L(\$)$$

When the wage is established in the labor market, households will supply labor until the marginal rate of substitution is equal to the wage, that is,

$$MRS_{Yl} = w$$

Since producers pay the same wage that households receive, the marginal rate of substitution of dollars (income) for leisure by households will be equated to the marginal dollar product of labor, that is,

$$MRS_{Yl} = w = MP_L(\$)$$

which is the marginal condition for global efficiency in the labor market.

Similarly, it can be shown that if an interest rate is established in the capital market that is the same for all lenders and borrowers, the marginal rate of substitution of future for present dollars by households will be equated to the marginal rate of transformation of future for present dollars by firms, since

$$MRS_{fp} = 1 + i = MRT_{fp}$$

Thus, in a market system, the marginal conditions for efficiency are satisfied in both factor markets and the markets for goods and services. The market mechanism itself ensures that there will be no excess demand for, or supply of, any good or service.

3-2 MARKET FAILURES

In the previous section we developed a market model that theoretically satisfies all the Paretian conditions for economic efficiency. Such a model is traditionally set forth to justify a market system as a means of efficient resource allocation.

Proponents of a market system and laissez faire public policy argue that the market mechanism will produce an equilibrium situation in which no one can be made better off without making someone else worse off. However, it is also well known that there are many cases in which an actual market system will not result in a welfare optimum. This is because the theoretical model contains certain implicit assumptions that are not always satisfied in the real world. In this section we examine some of these market failures.

Failure to Achieve Equilibrium

It was noted that the achievement of market equilibrium in which the quantity demanded equals the quantity supplied is necessary for global efficiency. An assumption implicit in our discussion of a market system is that market equilibrium will always be achieved within a reasonable time frame. Producers will respond to excess supply by lowering supply price, which will induce consumers to purchase more and hence clear the market. If there is excess demand, consumers will bid up prices to induce firms to increase supply. Thus prices are presumed to be flexible in any direction and producers' and consumers' responses to price changes are seen as being sufficiently rapid to clear the market within a reasonable period of time.

An example of the misapplication of this market model was the notion that the chronic unemployment of the 1930s could be remedied by following laissez faire policies. Traditional economists argued that if labor was in excess supply, workers would bid down wages, causing firms to hire more workers, thereby eliminating unemployment. Thus laissez faire would eventually result in a full employment equilibrium. John Maynard Keynes in his revolutionary treatise, *The General Theory of Employment, Interest, and Money,* pointed out that in a modern industrial economy wages tend to be inflexible in the downward direction. Furthermore, when demand is severely depressed, firms are likely to respond slowly, if at all, to lower factor prices. Keynes's famous statement, "In the long run we are dead," underscored the fact that the static analysis of markets ignores the amount of time required to achieve equilibrium.[1] A laissez faire policy might produce results in theory, but the amount of time required to achieve equilibrium is unspecified. Public policy must be addressed to eliminating unemployment immediately, not in fifty or one hundred years.

Other economists have pointed out limitations of the static analysis that assumes the economy is always in equilibrium.[2] A dynamic approach that looks at market behavior in the short run is essential for an examination of the welfare effects of a market system.

[1] This is an oversimplification of the Keynesian analysis of unemployment. For a fuller discussion see Nancy S. Barrett, *The Theory of Macroeconomic Policy* (Englewood Cliffs, N.J.: Prentice-Hall, 1972), chapters 8 and 9.

[2] See, for instance, Paul A. Samuelson, *Foundations of Economic Analysis* (Cambridge, Mass.: Harvard University Press, 1947), chapter 9.

The question of equilibrium analysis in economic theory is an important methodological issue that cannot be fully examined in the context of an overview of market failures. We will return to this issue in chapter 7.

Monopoly

A crucial assumption of the market model is that buyers and sellers act independently and that each is so small in relation to total market demand and supply that the purchases or sales of any one has a negligible effect on market prices.

This assumption flies in the face of the observed tendency in many markets for buyers or sellers to join together in an attempt to influence market prices. Each individual worker is small in relation to the total labor market, and his decision to work more or less has no impact on prevailing wages. Labor unions, however, can have a significant effect on market wages. By a collective decision to withhold labor in a strike or by restricting entry of workers into the market, unions can force firms to pay wages higher than would be established in the market model.

The unionization of labor in a market economy is the natural outgrowth of another phenomenon at odds with the assumptions of the model — the growth of firms to mammoth monoliths that account for such a large proportion of industry output that they can effectively control market prices by their decisions concerning how much to produce.[3]

What is the effect on the allocation of resources when a buyer or seller is large enough to influence market prices by his purchases or sales? Suppose the goal of the firm is to maximize profits. Just as in the previous analysis, the firm will expand output as long as the addition to revenue, marginal revenue (MR), exceeds the addition to cost, marginal cost, MC. If marginal cost increases with output, profit maximization occurs where

$$MR = MC$$

For the small firm whose output decisions cannot affect market price, MR is equal to price, that is,

$$MR = p$$

since the price is the change in revenue associated with selling one more unit. Such a firm can sell as much as it can produce at that price, and its demand curve, the relation between its output and potential selling price, is a horizontal line, as shown in Figure 3–1, intersecting the vertical axis at the prevailing market price, p_e. For such a firm, profit maximization occurs where price equals marginal cost, that is,

$$MR = p = MC$$

---

[3] John Kenneth Galbraith, *American Capitalism: The Theory of Countervailing Power* (Boston: Houghton Mifflin, 1956) discusses this tendency for units on one side of a market to join together in response to monopoly power on the other side.

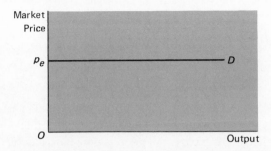

FIGURE 3–1
Relation Between Market Price and Output for a
Small Firm (Market Model)

Suppose, however, that the firm is so large that it can effect changes in market output that will influence price. As its output increases, it must lower its price to induce households to purchase the larger quantity. The demand curve for such a firm is shown in Figure 3–2. Notice that when the firm lowers its price in order to sell the increased output, it must reduce the price on *all* units. The change in revenue, for some change in output, therefore, is not reflected only in the unit price but includes the loss on all units sold when the price changes. Algebraically,

$$MR = \frac{\Delta TR}{\Delta q} = p + \left(\frac{\Delta p}{\Delta q}\right)q$$

where $\Delta p/\Delta q$ is the change in price associated with a change in output. Since the demand curve is negatively sloped, $\Delta p/\Delta q$ is negative and marginal revenue is less than price. As shown in Figure 3–2, for every level of output, marginal

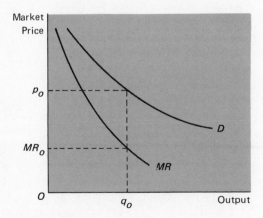

FIGURE 3–2
Relation Between Market Price and Output for a
Large Firm (Monopoly Model)

revenue lies below selling price (read from the demand curve). When output is q_o, selling price is p_o and marginal revenue is MR_o.

We noted earlier that a firm maximizing profit will set marginal revenue equal to marginal cost, that is,

$$MR = MC$$

Figure 3–3 shows that a firm large enough to affect market price by its output decisions (in this case a monopoly) will produce q_m (that output for which $MR = MC$) and charge a price p_m, the price at which q_m can be sold. Notice that the Pareto efficient output, q_e, is determined where the demand curve crosses the MC curve, since for q_e selling price p_e will equal marginal cost. Thus, if marginal revenue is less than price, q_m will be less than q_e, the Pareto efficient output, and p_m will be greater than p_e and greater than marginal cost.

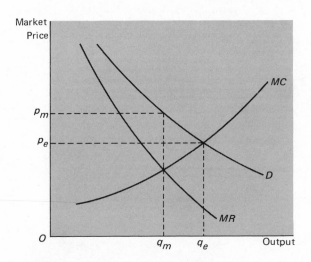

FIGURE 3–3
Monopoly Market Performance

Externalities

Externalities occur when there is a discrepancy between private and social benefits or costs associated with the consumption or production of some good or service.[4] When externalities exist, actions that would maximize private gains or minimize private losses are not generally consistent with social optima. Although

---

[4] The term *externality* refers to the fact that some good (external economy) or bad (external diseconomy) is generated by the consumer or producer that does not affect him or his decision, that is, the effect is external to his own welfare. Externalities, however, affect the welfare of others.

externalities represent a gain (benefit) or loss (cost), they are not taken into account by market participants and hence are not included in market values.

Consider the case of a rendering plant that produces tallow and emits an objectionable odor. For the owner of the plant the single output is tallow. For society there is a joint product, tallow and odor. Suppose, for simplicity, there is a single variable factor of production, labor. Then the private production function is

$$T = f(L)$$

where T is tallow output and L is labor input. The private marginal product of labor is

$$MP_L^P = \frac{\Delta T}{\Delta L}$$

The social production function is

$$O + T = g(L)$$

where O is odor output.[5]

Now suppose that the odor emitted depends on the level of tallow production, that is,

$$O = h(T)$$

Then the social marginal product of labor is

$$MP_L^S = \frac{\Delta(T + O)}{\Delta L}$$

$$= \frac{\Delta T}{\Delta L} + \frac{\Delta O}{\Delta L}$$

$$= \frac{\Delta T}{\Delta L} + \left(\frac{\Delta O}{\Delta T} \times \frac{\Delta T}{\Delta L}\right)$$

$$= \frac{\Delta T}{\Delta L}\left(1 + \frac{\Delta O}{\Delta T}\right)$$

$$= MP_L^P\left(1 + \frac{\Delta O}{\Delta T}\right)$$

The ratio $\Delta O/\Delta T$ is called the **interaction effect.** The greater the interaction, the greater the discrepancy between marginal social product and marginal private product of labor.

We know that the firm will hire workers until the value of the marginal product of labor is equal to the wage. If p_T is the market price of tallow, this implies

$$MVP_L^P = p_T \times MP_L^P = w$$

---

[5] The unit in which O is measured is immaterial, provided a link is established between O and social welfare.

where MVP_L^P is the private marginal value product of labor. For a social optimum, the value of the marginal social product of labor must equal the wage. If p_O is the social value of a unit of odor, then the value of the marginal social product, MVP_L^S, is

$$MVP_L^S = p_T \frac{\Delta T}{\Delta L} + p_O \left(\frac{\Delta O}{\Delta T} \times \frac{\Delta T}{\Delta L} \right)$$

$$= p_T \frac{\Delta T}{\Delta L} \left[1 + \left(\frac{p_O}{p_T} \times \frac{\Delta O}{\Delta T} \right) \right]$$

$$= MVP_L^P \left[1 + \left(\frac{p_O}{p_T} \times \frac{\Delta O}{\Delta T} \right) \right]$$

and the social optimum occurs where

$$MVP_L^S = MVP_L^P \left[1 + \left(\frac{p_O}{p_T} \times \frac{\Delta O}{\Delta T} \right) \right] = w$$

Since odor represents a loss in utility, p_O must be negative, so that

$$MVP_L^S < MVP_L^P$$

Figure 3–4 shows the social and private demand for labor in tallow production and the associated private and social optimal levels of employment for a fixed wage. When the wage is w, L_p units will be employed. However, L_s is the socially optimum level of employment in tallow production. Thus private decisions result in overemployment in the tallow industry and an oversupply of tallow.

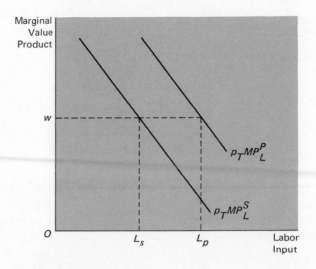

FIGURE 3–4
Private and Social Employment Optima in the Presence of an
External Diseconomy

Suppose the production process generates a good rather than a bad. Professor James Meade cites the example of an apple farmer who generates an externality to a neighboring beekeeper in the form of nectar.[6] Bees produce more honey, the more nectar they obtain from apple blossoms. In this case, the marginal social value product of labor in apple production, MVP_{LA}^S, is

$$MVP_{LA}^S = MVP_{LA}^P\left[1 + \left(\frac{p_H}{p_A} \times \frac{\Delta H}{\Delta A}\right)\right]$$

where p_A is the price of apples, p_H is the price of honey, MVP_{LA}^P is the marginal private value product of labor in apple production, and $\Delta H/\Delta A$ is the interaction effect on honey production of apple production.

Since p_H and p_A are greater than zero, the marginal social product of labor in apple production exceeds the marginal private product. As shown in Figure 3–5,

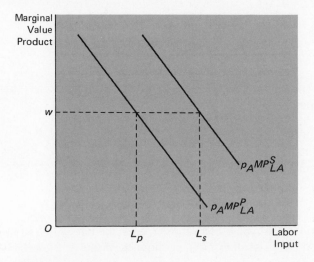

FIGURE 3–5
Private and Social Employment Optima in the Presence of an External Economy

private profit maximization results in less labor employed in apple production, L_p, than is socially optimal, L_s, and a consequent underproduction of apples.

Another type of externality occurs when there is a negative interaction effect on one good when another is produced. One frequently cited example is the factory smokestack that belches soot onto the clean linen of the neighboring laundry.

In all these cases, there is a discrepancy between social and private costs and benefits associated with a particular activity. Since market values reflect private

[6] Economic Journal, LXII (March 1952), pp. 54–67. This example is also cited in Francis M. Bator, "The Anatomy of Market Failure," Quarterly Journal of Economics, LXXII (August 1958), pp. 351–379.

costs and benefits, they understate (in the case of activities generating external economies) and overstate (in the case of activities generating external diseconomies) true social values. If a price system could be devised that would reflect social values, it would produce optimal social decisions. An attempt to devise such a price system is at the heart of tax-subsidy schemes that would purportedly remedy the effect of externalities on market decisions.

Suppose we were to place a per unit tax t on tallow production such that

$$t = -p_O \times \frac{\Delta O}{\Delta T}$$

where p_O is the social value of the odor produced by the rendering plant, O is the odor output, and T is the tallow output. If such a tax were imposed, the private marginal value product of labor in tallow production would be

$$MVP_L^P = (p_T - t)\frac{\Delta T}{\Delta L}$$

$$= p_T \frac{\Delta T}{\Delta L}\left[1 + \left(\frac{p_O}{p_T} \times \frac{\Delta O}{\Delta T}\right)\right] = MVP_L^S$$

That is, the private marginal value product would exactly equal the social marginal value product and hence

$$MVP_L^P = MVP_L^S = w$$

Optimal private decisions would coincide with optimal social decisions.

Equivalently, subsidies of an amount

$$S = p_Y \times \frac{\Delta Y}{\Delta X}$$

where p_Y is the social value of Y, and $\Delta Y/\Delta X$ is the interaction of Y with X, could be provided in the cases of external economies, where Y, a good, is produced external to the production of X.

Public Goods

The most extreme case of an externality is a pure **public good.** Samuelson defines a pure public good as one for which total social consumption is the same as each person's consumption. If Y is total consumption of a public good, then

$$Y = Y_1 = Y_2 = \cdots = Y_n$$

where Y_i is consumption of the good by the ith individual.[7] National defense and programs to eliminate air pollution are examples of public goods and services

---

[7] Paul A. Samuelson, "Diagrammatic Exposition of a Theory of Public Expenditures," *Review of Economics and Statistics, XXXVII* (November 1955), pp. 350–356.

available to everyone in equal amounts. Cleaner air benefits everyone, and one person cannot increase his consumption of clean air at another's expense.

On the other hand, total social consumption of a private good, X, is the sum of each person's consumption of it, that is,

$$X = Y_1 + X_2 + \cdots + X_n$$

where X_i is consumption by the ith individual. If one person consumes a private good such as food, clothing, or an automobile, he prevents another from consuming it.

Mixed public goods partake of some aspects of public and private goods. Although many people benefit from the provision of these goods, the amount one consumes may affect another's ability to consume the good. Education, public transportation, spectator sports activities are mixed public goods. Two people can enjoy a lecture, but its effectiveness is reduced if the room becomes very crowded. Thus the entry of one more person may reduce the benefits to others in the room. For simplicity we will assume that goods are either purely public or purely private. The application to mixed public goods follows directly from this analysis.

When a private good is produced, it is consumed by a single individual. Thus that individual's private gain from consuming that good, reflected in his marginal rate of substitution of that good for other goods, is equal to the social gain. Assuming the social cost is reflected in the marginal rate of transformation (there are no production externalities), it follows that a social optimum occurs where

$$MRS = MRT$$

and where

$$MRS_1 = MRS_2 = \cdots = MRS_n$$

MRS_i being the marginal rate of substitution of the public good for other goods for the ith consumer.

For public goods, which everyone consumes equally (your war is my war, and so on), the social gain from the production of one or more unit is the *sum* of the marginal rates of substitution for all individuals in the economy. Thus it follows that allocation of resources to public goods is socially optimal where

$$MRS_1 + MRS_2 + \cdots + MRS_n = MRT$$

For optimal allocation of resources to public goods the sum of the individual marginal rates of substitution must be equated to their marginal rate of transformation. Consequently, a private market system in which individuals adjust their purchases and producers adjust production so that

$$MRS_{YX} = \frac{p_X}{p_Y} = MRT_{YX}$$

will necessarily underproduce Y. That is, private decisions will result in less public Y and more private X than is socially optimal. In terms of the externality discussion, social value exceeds private value to the greatest possible extent. That is why public goods can be viewed as the extreme externality.

A price system alone is not adequate to ensure optimal provision of public goods. Neither is the sort of generalized subsidy scheme applicable in the case of production externalities.[8] Notice that each individual at the margin has the same subjective rate of trade-off of a private good for other goods. Thus, charging fixed prices (or prices plus fixed subsidy) for the good will be sufficient to produce this result. However, individuals can and generally do consume public goods where, at the margin, the subjective rate of exchange with private goods varies among consumers. Since all individuals must consume equal amounts of the public good, Y, then on the average the marginal rate of substitution of public for private goods (the amount of public goods required to "compensate" the consumer for giving up private goods) will be lower for those consuming more private goods, the rich. If consumer I has more private goods than consumer II, that is,

$$X_I > X_{II}$$

it is likely that

$$MRS_{YX}^I < MRS_{YX}^{II}$$

Consumers will be satisfied with the amount of public goods provided as long as

$$MRS_{YX} = \frac{p_X}{p_Y}$$

Since individuals have different MRS_{YX} for any level of Y, then unless individuals are charged different prices for public goods, efficient allocation of resources to public goods will not occur. If MRS_{YX} declines, on the average, with the level of income, taxes should be higher at higher income levels.[9] However, for true efficiency each household should be charged a different price for public goods, since MRS_{YX} will vary among households depending upon individual tastes as well as income levels. To establish such a price system would be a practical impossibility, since it requires a knowledge of the subjective preferences of each consumer in the economy. This was not the case for private goods, for which fixed prices ensured that the efficiency condition

$$MRS_{XY}^I = \frac{p_Y}{p_X} = MRS_{XY}^{II}$$

---

[8] The external effect in the case of public goods comes from the consumption side. The examples in the previous section were of production externalities.

[9] Here is an argument for income taxation based on the criterion of efficiency alone. Arguments for income taxation are generally concerned with distributive questions. While most people can agree on the desirability of efficiency, there is likely to be considerable disagreement on the optimal income distribution, and consequently arguments based on efficiency are often more powerful than those based on distributional equity.

would be satisfied. Consumers will automatically adjust their purchases to satisfy the efficiency condition.

If a price system were used to assure efficient allocation of resources to public goods, consumers would not reveal their preferences or, equivalently, the amount they would be willing to pay for public goods, since they could enjoy the full amount of Y regardless of how much they paid for it. To the extent that some public goods are not *pure* public goods (for example, highways, schools), this statement must be qualified. In all cases, however, the social benefit exceeds the benefit to the individual, and hence the individual cannot be forced to pay the full amount of what he enjoys.

To summarize, given the discrepancy between social benefit and individual private benefit associated with public goods, a market system will underproduce public goods. Furthermore, any attempt to finance public goods on the basis of prices charged to users would fail. Consequently, the public sector finances such activities from tax revenues raised on the basis of other criteria.[10]

Income Distribution

A Pareto optimum is attained when no one can be made better off without making someone else worse off. Since there is a different Pareto optimum associated with every conceivable distribution of welfare, and assuming a direct relation between welfare and income, the Pareto criterion clearly skirts the issue of the optimal income distribution.[11]

Figure 3-6 shows a utility trade-off frontier between two individuals or, alternatively, between one individual and everyone else taken together. Points on the frontier, such as A, represent a Pareto optimum, since U_I, the utility of individual I, can only be increased at the expense of the utility of individual II, U_{II}. On the other hand, points inside the frontier, such as B, are inefficient, since U_I can be increased by moving to A without reducing U_{II}, that is, without making individual II worse off. Alternatively, a move from B to C would make II better off without making I worse off.

The Pareto optimum can be viewed as the best allocation of resources *for any given income distribution*. The question of the "best" income distribution, however, requires the sort of interpersonal value judgment associated with robbing Peter to pay Paul. Consequently, many economists have considered such judgments beyond their scope. Others base criteria for optimal income distribution on theoretical arguments.

For instance, if we assume that for higher income levels the gain in utility

---

[10] Criteria most commonly put forward for taxation are neutrality with respect to the price system, distributional equity, ability to pay, and the benefit principle. For a discussion see Richard A. Musgrave, *The Theory of Public Finance* (New York: McGraw-Hill, 1959), chapters 4 and 5.

[11] Economic welfare increases with the consumption of goods as well as of leisure. If low incomes are associated with a high consumption of leisure, then there is not necessarily a positive relation between income and welfare. If a measure of income is to reflect welfare, it should include leisure. Also, there are welfare effects associated with different types of work that should be taken into account.

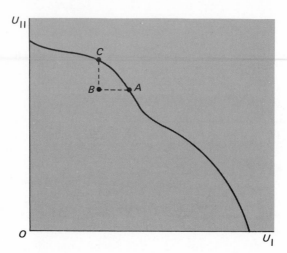

FIGURE 3–6
A Utility Trade-Off Frontier

associated with a $1 increment in income is lower than at low levels of income, then redistribution of income toward greater equality is viewed as desirable on the basis of the principle of maximizing social welfare. Such a conclusion still requires interpersonal comparisons, however. Although for each individual the marginal utility of income may fall, as in Figure 3–7,[12] it is not necessarily true that the marginal utility of income for some high-income individual (or for that matter, all high-income persons taken together) is any smaller than that for low-income individuals. The latter involves comparing the psychic satisfaction experienced by different individuals.

Income Distribution in a Market System

A competitive market model, in the absence of externalities, will produce a Pareto optimal allocation of resources, but that allocation may produce a distribution of income that is viewed (at least by some observers) as undesirable. In a market model the return to factors of production will equal their marginal value product as perceived by their employers.

Firms will employ productive factors until their marginal value product equals the factor price, that is, until

---

[12] It is not obvious that the marginal utility of income should decline at higher income levels. We generally assume that the marginal utility of consuming a *single good* falls as more is consumed, because of a "saturation effect." But it doesn't necessarily follow that given the large variety of goods and services available, marginal utility will fall as more of all of these is consumed. Marginal utility of income could conceivably rise as the life style improves, at least up to a certain point. A welfare family, discouraged and pessimistic, may incur less psychic satisfaction from a $100 windfall than the same family in more affluent days, when it is upwardly mobile, with aspirations of achieving middle-class status.

The Day Before

Also by Dick Allen

Ode to the Cold War: Poems New and Selected (1997)
Flight and Pursuit (1987)
Overnight in the Guest House of the Mystic (1984)
Regions with No Proper Names (1975)
Anon and Various Time Machine Poems (1971)

The Day Before

NEW POEMS Dick Allen

Sarabande Books

LOUISVILLE, KENTUCKY

No part of this book may be reproduced without written permission of the publisher. Please direct inquiries to:

> Managing Editor
> Sarabande Books, Inc.
> 2234 Dundee Road, Suite 200
> Louisville, KY 40205

Library of Congress Cataloging-in-Publication Data

Allen, Dick, 1939–
    The day before : new poems / by Dick Allen.— 1st ed.
    p. cm.
    ISBN 1-889330-75-2 (hardcover : alk. paper) — ISBN 1-889330-76-0 (pbk. : alk. paper) I. Title.
PS3551.L3922 D39 2003
811'.54—dc21   2002007225

Cover image: *Spring Turning*, by Grant Wood. Oil masonite panel, 1936.
© Estate of Grant Wood/Licensed by VAGA, New York, NY.

Cover and text design by Charles Casey Martin.

Manufactured in the United States of America.
This book is printed on acid-free paper.

Sarabande Books is a nonprofit literary organization.

 This project is supported in part by an award from the National Endowment for the Arts, and by the Kentucky Arts Council, a state agency of the Education, Arts, and Humanities Cabinet.

FIRST EDITION

in the memory of Lucy Allen Heath

TABLE OF CONTENTS

Acknowledgments . . . . *xi*

"And Leave My Human Feelings..." . . . . *xv*

ONE

A Boy Called Vanish 3

Homefront 4

Triptych 6

The Father Suite

    Steady as She Goes 10

    Heart Condition 13

    Breath 14

    Those Who Are Surpassed 15

Bishop Eyes 18

"God Gives to Every Bird..." 20

After Reading Tichborne's Elegy 22

The Children 25

TWO

Zen Living 29

Intuition 30

In Wyeth Country 31

Rime Forest 32

Ferns 34

Strip Malls 36

Quiet, Quiet Now 37

The Simile 38

The Green Children 39

The American Zen Master 41

Cassandra in Connecticut 44

April 45

The Selfishness of the Poetry Reader 47

The Devotion of Thomas Merton 49

Memo from the Desk of Wallace Stevens: 51

Vehicle 53

THREE

The Familiar 57

On Roark's Farm 58

Letter to One Who May Be Dead or Not 60

Urban Pastoral 62

Sunday 65

A Shadowy Government Agency 66

Some Man I Knew 68

The Back of God 71

Animus 72

After a Proverb by William Blake 73

[Say We Have to Name the World Again] 74

If You Get There Before I Do 75

Then 78

FOUR

The Cove 81

The Day Before Yesterday 83

Lost Friends 87

Being Taught 90

Jubilate 93

Letter to Ye Feng, His Student Now in Iowa 95

Poem for Li, in Her White Bridal Dress 97

Texas Prison Town 99

Man of the Cloth 102

Although the Temporal Is Beautiful 104

Poem for My Sixtieth Birthday 106

The Litany of Disparagement 109

This Far 111

The Author *115*

ACKNOWLEDGMENTS

Grateful acknowledgement is given to the editors and publishers of the following, in which some of these poems first appeared, a few in slightly different versions:

American Arts Quarterly, "And Leave My Human Feelings...," "Rime Forest"

The Antioch Review, "[Say We Have to Name the World Again]"

Atlanta Review, "In Wyeth Country," "Jubilate"

The Atlantic Monthly, "Memo from the Desk of Wallace Stevens," Part II of "The Litany of Disparagement"

The Bible of Hell (Pendragonian Publications, 2000), "The Back of God"

Boulevard, "Lost Friends"

The Café Review, "The Selfishness of the Poetry Reader"

The Cortland Review, "Poem for My Sixtieth Birthday"

Crab Orchard Review, "On Roark's Farm," "Sunday"

Family Reunion: Poems by Parents of Grown Children (Chicory Blue Press, 2003), "The Children"

The Gettysburg Review, "The Father Suite," "Some Man I Knew"

Hampden-Sydney Poetry Review, "Urban Pastoral"

The Hudson Review, "The Cove," "Letter to Ye Feng, His Student Now in Iowa," "Poem for Li in Her White Bridal Dress"

Image: A Journal of the Arts and Religion, "The Devotion of
Thomas Merton"

*Intelligence There with Passion: A Festschrift in Honor of Frederick
Morgan's Fiftieth Anniversary at* The Hudson Review (Aralia
Press, 1998), "Intuition"

Margie, "A Shadowy Government Agency"

Mid-American Review, "The Simile"

The New Criterion, "The Familiar," "Ferns," "Homefront"

The New Republic, "Then"

North American Review, "Letter to One Who May Be Dead
or Not"

The Ontario Review, "Triptych," "This Far"

*Photographers, Writers, and the American Scene: Visions of
Passage* (Arena Editons, 2002), "The Day Before Yesterday,"
"Quiet, Quiet Now"

Pivot, "Animus," "The Green Children"

Ploughshares, "Cassandra in Connecticut"

Poetry, "The American Zen Master," "Being Taught," "God Gives
to Every Bird . . . ," "Man of the Cloth," "Texas Prison Town,"
"Zen Living"

Poetry Review (England), "Although the Temporal is Beautiful"

Quarterly West, "If You Get There Before I Do," "Vehicle"

Rosebud, "April"

Salmagundi, "After Reading Tichborne's Elegy"

Smartish Pace, "After a Proverb by William Blake," "Bishop Eyes"

The Yale Review, "A Boy Called Vanish"

"The Cove" was reprinted in *The Best American Poetry: 1998*.

"The Selfishness of the Poetry Reader" was reprinted in *The Best American Poetry: 1999*.

"The American Zen Master," "Simile," "God Gives to Every Bird ...," and "Vehicle" were reprinted on *Poetry Daily*.

"And Leave My Human Feelings..."

The world, as we know it, will cease to exist,
Schrödinger's cat will live / Schrödinger's cat will die.
The towers on the rock will turn to mist.

An open palm is hidden by a fist,
And what screamed here is not what happened by.
The world, as we know it, will cease to exist.

Amethyst to coal, and coal to amethyst.
That dragon in the field's no dragonfly.
The towers on the rock will turn to mist.

The heart of each life's story is its sudden twist.
Even the dullest child can grow a weather eye.
The world, as we know it, will cease to exist.

When thwarted lover turns to terrorist,
Perverting God to set himself On High,
The towers on the rock will turn to mist.

Backlist, checklist, snake hiss, deathlist.
I saw a huge 11 fall down from the sky.
The world, as we know it, will cease to exist.
The towers on the rock will turn to mist.

And these ideas, which constitute reality, are names, as nominalism showed. Not that they may not be more than names, but that they are nothing less than names. Language is that which gives us reality, and not as a mere vehicle of reality, but as its true flesh.... And thus logic operates upon aesthetics, the concept upon the expression, upon the word....

Language and Philosophers
Miguel De Unamuno Y Jungo

ONE

A Boy Called Vanish

He was about drainpipes, spyglasses, red Pegasus
on a Mobil sign,
and knew, as other boys didn't, he was vanishing
like the first innings of a baseball game,
but couldn't stop it. He was about
how you count to ten and look around
for nobody there. While everyone slept,
he wound his wristwatch backward and uncombed his hair,
whispering *"Shazam! Shazam!"* He wore
brown corduroy pants; he lost
footprints in the snow across the fields
to black and white birches. To see him,
you had to be as careful as a lock and key
or the soul of forgiveness. Everyone else
saw only that he wasn't them and turned their heads
into their sorrows. He collected
moods of small houses, ripples on the lake,
and when he bicycled the evening roads,
old Fords up on blocks and backyard girls
clinging to their mothers' hands. He was
watching himself vanish into me
and hated but accepted how I gave him books
to speed him on his way,
and my dog Buck to guard him from all harm.

Homefront

Sunflowers grew so tall in the Coshburns' garden,
ten, twelve feet before a night windstorm
flattened them, decapitating some
(whose heads we found floating in the road,
and dangling from the wire mesh of a rabbit warren),
they frightened us...as if they were children who become
adults too soon, the darkness at their roots
sensed by other children—as I remember
sensing the coming beauty of Nancy Parker,
the death of Billy Meade. The sunflowers
grew uglier and uglier, a dozen higher ones
with faces descending at us from between
invisible shoulders, faces grotesquely swaying
on horrible stalks. And yet the Coshburns
seemed not to notice. Blithely, they beckoned us
closer and closer. Look up and see the sun,
they said. Don't you wish that you and you
could grow so tall. The night they fell,
moths bumped our windowscreens, the radio
went static, then dead. My mother screamed
at her clothesline. From the upstairs porch
of our summer cottage, lightning serifs melting
all over the sky, I watched the Coshburns' garden
as the sunflowers, one by one, went down,
splayed like compass points; and I was glad
the forces beyond us were protecting us

even in the small towns of upstate New York,
in 1945, in that hot war-torn July.

Triptych

I

The lake beyond the two boys playing basketball
   does not shimmer. It's simply a gray wash
below a few unfocused hills
   so low and commonplace no one's yet named them,
and the house in the foreground, with the old
   Dodge up on blocks beside it isn't worth
even a glance. Why enter it? Inside,
   the mirrors will be dusty, the furniture a few
dark pieces scattered on some thin gray rugs,
   nothing that would make you climb the stairs
to the bedroom in back, its single window
   facing the lake, beneath it an old half-rotted
picnic table salvaged from a dump, the circular
   clothesline in a square of ragged bushes....
Yet this isn't poverty. The boys are fed
   sufficiently, and loved. The roads
you can't see joining other roads
   are passable, the cities at their ends—
thick airstrips leading off to Vietnam,
   Nicaragua hot beneath the moon—
no dream. All reaches and is reached from here,
   even on this day my father stands outside
and lifts his Kodak, takes his undistinguished
   photograph of house and car and lake and bare

tree branches cluttering, haphazardly, the white
    November sky. And like an afterthought
or because they happened to be there,
    too small and distant to be waved away,
two boys.

      II

        What were his thoughts? What were
my mother's thoughts outside her magazine
    ambitions for her sons? *Gray Saturdays.*
The radiator cat. Schoolboy friends
    killed at Normandy. The never-ending wish
and want! When the lake froze over
    we'd walk a mile across it toward the dark
and gutted icehouse. "Listen!" my father would shout
    into a broken window. *Listen, listen . . . listen*
his voice would echo. Then retracing
    our snowcrust path, we made our way out on
the lake again, ice booming, and the mist
    of slight wind-scattered snow so gossamer
we'd lift our mittened hands to part it constantly.
    White eyebrows and hot cocoa and the game of Clue
my mother always won. All reaches. All is reached
    from here. Chernobyl. The fattened goosenecked cloud
of the Challenger. Nixon waving. Dallas.
    Press of fingers on computer buttons.
The Chinese horns and hellgates of Korea.

Hiroshima. Dresden. "The Eyes and Ears of the World."
The Holocaust.... You touch my arm
    to bring me out of it. Dulled, dazed,
approaching sixty with my hands still balancing
    a basketball, knees bent, my eyes
sighting to the hole in space above the rim,
    I fire. The world arcs up. My father fires....

III

    Listen, listen...listen
his voice would echo. But for what? For why?
    Not even half a century has passed since I
first heard him shouting in those charred-wood rafters
    and the booming of the ice, the fleck, fleck
of dry snow scraped by boots—and one day for an hour
    with my Gilbert microscope upon the picnic table,
I tested the hypothesis of no
    snowflake shaped the same—and in that world
of crystal symmetry, found such elegance
    and mystery I thought I might reach God
through search, not prayer. Mistake. How blurred
    was my belief.... In the photograph
two edges and one chimney of the cottages
    whose lots touched ours; a section of the fence
around the village's cracked tennis court;
    a streetlamp that will soon come on,
the boys will stand beneath. They'll toss

8

the basketball, bounce-pass it, dribble it
until their hands are raw. No one will take
    their picture at this hour—soon not even they
remember what they say: passing the ball, brilliantly
    catching it behind their backs and whipping it
away, away. Up to the moon. Up to the stars,
    away, away.... When they're gone
perhaps it rains or snows. Ice freezes
    on every twig and branch, catching the streetlamp's glow
in such a way a web of light is spun
    around it until dawn. No color in the frame.
November day, then night.... Two boys playing ball.

The Father Suite

I. Steady as She Goes

"Steady as she goes," my father would yell,
Steering the boat we rented that only summer
He had any money,
Between the buoys and the other, larger

Boats all around us. His bald head covered
With a skipper's cap, its emblem
A small gold anchor on a field of black,
He'd stand at the helm

Laughing for dear life. "Steady as she goes,
Steady as she goes." The ocean
He sailed us out on, I remember to this day,
Was calm as a silver coin

Near the shore, but roughened out deeper,
Waves melting and reforming lee and starboard,
Bow and aft. "Beautiful, beautiful, beautiful,"
He'd say. Then toward

Noon he'd becalm us. From an icy chest,
Red pop and sandwiches, their crusts
Meant to be torn off
And thrown to any gulls at rest

On the sea's path.... The next year,
Back in poverty's pit, a tenement
Of boarded windows, light bulbs hung from cords,
Where my mother scrubbed dirt from dirt and found more dirt,

He'd sit backward on his kitchen chair
And staring out at a clothesline fat with clothes,
Pretend, with us, they were sails
Filled with wind blows

As the blue sheets billowed and the thin skirts spun
Around on their hangers. "Steady as she goes," he'd whisper,
"Steady as she goes"—but not sorry for himself.
Don't think that, ever. I remember

When everything ached in him—you could hear it
In his voice and feel it in his arms
Trying to hug us goodnight, but clutching
Instead—he'd still not damn

The world, nor himself, nor us....
Why is life
So cruel? Surely it has a heart, but why's that heart
So punctured and ruptured? If

The breaks had gone right... but they didn't. If
He hadn't had children.... Out on that boat
When evening started to come and the lighthouse blinked
From the shore, like a tiny star in a net

Of low-lying clouds, he'd grow so silent
Looking down at us, feet spread to keep his balance,
It was as if his mind was lost, he'd never
Get us back home. But then he'd wince

Abruptly, shake his head from side to side
And find his voice again.... I've caught myself
Doing the same thing lately. It's
Just that there's so much grief

About, and to deal with—beauty and grief. I can't
Reconcile them well.... Slowly, not more than a quarter-inch
Over stalling speed, he'd steer us in,
Calling to other skippers, his nautical speech

Too proud to be rusty. "Steady as she goes," he'd sing
To the harbor and gas pumps and piers
We passed. To the wind-bent trees
In the coves, the houses and flashy cars

On the last viaduct we barely floated under
Before we docked. "Steady as she goes,"
He'd say one more time, after we'd tied
The ropes taut, and carefully hosed

Down the decks. Then, grandly sweeping his cap
As he bowed like an English admiral courting a lady,

He'd have our mother walk before him up the wooden ramp
To the parking lot. Gladly, he'd follow.... Gladly,

And I think knowingly, he burned his money up
That summer. "Good day, really good day,"
I can still hear him saying as he drove
Our ripped-seat Studebaker with its gray

Half-working dashboard
Into the city, holding an even thirty-six
Miles-per-hour because of, or despite
The eternally heavy traffic

Veering around us.... Beauty and grief, or maybe you
Can find some other words. Was it a foolish pose
Or blend of risk and caring? Does it matter which?
He kept our life here steady, steady as she goes.

II. Heart Condition

"You would take their side!" my mother screamed
    at my father
when the ambulance he'd finally summoned came,
    and she kicked and bit as they took her

from Aspinwall Drive,
    where she'd been trying to compel her heart back,

keep it alive

    on a diet of carrot sticks

and her famous will power. Tied down, sedated,

    eight hours later, she died.

Her heart literally burst. He'd waited

    and he'd cried

in her hospital room, begging to her, but she never

    spoke to him again,

went out of this world blaming others,

    scorning *that man*

who as she'd bloated then terribly thinned gave up

    his own life to help her plan

how she'd recover—she, a typical Bishop;

    and he, a typical Allen.

III. Breath

"He walked out on the prairie and he shot himself,"

    his wife said.

"Brains all over. Blood.

I think now I'll travel.... "

"Another life," writes my father, "gone with the wind,

    to cite Margaret Mitchell.

14

I always liked that title.
Your mother read that book from start to end

again and again." He's moved up to Idaho—
after her death—starting over,
living close to my brother.
This summer in the mountains he found heavy snow

blocking the road and backed his Jeep a mile
before he could turn.
He's given up trying to learn
to follow her principles

of good diet, proper dress—his hearing aid
often turned off.
He's been "a good boy" long enough,
he says, and too often afraid.

His emphysemic neighbor in the next-door condominium
told him he hadn't slept
for three nights running, then kept
his promise to himself to end the pain,

left his nose-tubes and his oxygen at home,
walked out on the prairie
that morning, very early.
"The day," my father says, "was a very pretty one."

IV. Those Who Are Surpassed

"Their eyes are always bigger than their stomachs,"
my father said,
"that's how you can tell them: big eyes,
little thin stomachs.

"At the table of life
they always heap too much and never finish."
Not him.
His plate was always cleared, he always kept

just a little room left over for dessert: Bavarian
creme pies,
deep dark chocolate cakes,
syrup floating up the edges of bread puddings,

and smacked his lips and seemed content, while those
around him groaned
and nibbled with embarrassment the rich
concoctions he'd planned for

with calculating visions and a loosened belt. "You see,
the secret's in the appetite," he said, "to know
what's possible
and what's impractical. One taste at a time,"

he said, "one delicious bite and savor it, and then
the next,"

who lived to ninety, gained tremendous girth
and died without a speck

of usual regret—his several books, his articles, his meals
completed in a lonely condominium in Idaho,
the dishes washed,
and he asleep within his great armchair.

Bishop Eyes

"Yes, he's ours, he has them," I remember
Grandmother Sadie (on my mother's side)
exclaim while leaning over our new son,
"the Bishop eyes."

My wife—three-quarters Slavic, great-great-great
granddaughter of a Russian countess—sighed
and rolled her own. In her family line
the Tartars and the Mongols always vied

in each new child—first one
emerging, then the other, in haphazard leaps
down through the genes. "You see,
the slant, the lovely almond shape,"

Grandmother Sadie said. "The girls
will all be after him." Somewhere,
some deep dark somewhere in our family tree,
a concubine from Canton or perhaps

a disgraced Peking lady from an outcast clan
that for a decade once ruled dynasties,
must have entered us, as if—truly—yes
her eyes became "the Bishop eyes"—and I've

seen them also in my uncles and my cousins' sons
(the gene is male and dominant and skips
generations as it runs). So I've come
also to believe

the Bishop eyes will last—no matter what
attacks them from the West.
The woman carried in them won't stay hidden
or suppressed

but looking up into our Occidental skies
shall find bronze doors of temples in the clouds,
brushstrokes and the missionary tracts,
then be cast down

and out...through my son...and in turn
his male grandchild, *ad infinitum*,
at their puzzled mothers holding them,
bemused and graced by mysteries they'd borne...

and Grandmother Sadie cooed, and wiggling her
arthritic fingers said again,
"Bishop eyes. Blue almonds. All the same,
those Bishop eyes."

"God Gives to Every Bird Its Proper Food but They Must All Fly for It"

My aunt, drowning in birdcalls, telephones
to say a wren has built its nest within
the little thoughts of her TV. A cardinal
is flying backward through her porcelain

and she can't stand it. Sparrows
have found the seeds among her early days;
a plover's lit upon her love of Charlotte Brontë,
her kitchen's filled with hopping chickadees,

what should she do? In her weakened state,
she cannot shoo them from their scurrying
across her long-held views and windowsills,
and one is pulling at her last heartstring

as if it's just some worm come out in the rain,
forced up from the soil in search of warmth.
A hawk is diving toward her Wyeth plate,
two grackles bite a prejudice to death

and even as she speaks, a mockingbird
is making toward her bed. My aunt,
who played the violin for Bernstein once,
adored his eyebrows and his stiff starched pants,

rode in rumble seats, and thought she saw
Picasso in a brothel sipping chocolate shakes,
has no will left, she says. The mourning doves
have claimed her closets for their own. Pine Siskins take

liberties, such liberties. A thousand miles away,
I hold the hambone into which she weeps,
and hear, behind her voice, the purple finch,
the evening grosbeak, and the rapt bluejays.

After Reading Tichborne's Elegy

The world shrinks to a face within a face,
The kind you sometimes see on the evening news
Bearded with microphones, its outer outline
Almost the same as yours, but behind it
Eyes that have seen the death of children, villages
Rubbled in hours, a mouth too slack to scream,
The face of our time. You look away. After all,
Pain is a commonplace and you have felt it
Often enough in your life—if not at this
Blanked-out intensity, still you have watched
Presidents go down on the sidewalks, ambulances
Traveling dark roads, and heard in the night wind
Wings beating, and shrieking of something caught
Too small to matter. Often, your living room
Seems lighted by pitch-pine torches, the interior
Of an Egyptian burial chamber, all the things you love
At hand: perfumes, paintings, flasks of wine,
Tablets of chants and prayers. Such richness would
Appall the ancient kings.... You rise from your couch,
Seeing the face again. In the golden light
It floats and weeps. If you could speak to it
You might ask forgiveness, but it does not see you
Or your awkwardness. Once, when you were walking
A low road through the Scottish moors, you found
Concealed by heather, a face with a child's puffed cheeks
Carved on a wayside stone, and an inscription

Too blurred to read except for the words *Jesu*
And *Merci*. The larks cried overhead; you kept
So still you could almost make out human speech
Among them. And then a storm like a clothed fist
Struck at you, you hurried on toward the village
Through gusts of warm rain.... You think of strangers,
Thousands of them, passing you in a mall,
Cirrus clouds laid low, each one that passes,
A tiny mystery: you are walking
Constantly through their slowly moving edges
As they are through yours. What is required,
Or if not required, allowed? And if you have
The will to change the world, yet lack the power,
Are you accomplished in the eyes of God?
In the cedars of Lebanon, the face appears;
And it is looking from a second-story window
Over the Harlem River; and it is in a snowstorm
Beating on Afghanistan. So is it too
On the movie screen of a bird-beaked Concorde above
The Pacific, reflects from silvered glasses
Worn on the Riviera. Always, it stares through you
And you grow dizzy with too much reproach and grasp
The fireplace mantel for balance while the vase
Of butterfly weed, daisies, clover, black-eyed Susans
Trembles before you. To take all this in!
And you think of Tichborne writing in his tower,
Of his darkened hourglass, his unspun thread,
The dawn come like a boat upon the Thames.
World images replace the limited

Visions of your country torn halfway apart
As you turn the cable channels, finding one
Ashen and silent. You stare into its gray
Face, for in the static say astronomers
Are signals from the time the universe
Began. On this dark planet, kneeling here,
You tune the voices other beings may
Have traveled on, until the algebraic storm
Crests upon you and you lift your head
Once more from all things asking you to live
For those who suffer, all who speak no longer
Of terror, wonder, and you see upon the wall
Your print of Wood's *Stone City* where a man
Rides a huge white dray beside a windmill
Still as everything the artist froze to stone:
Stone bridge, stone river, and great fields of stone
That will not break though you must strike at them.
Strike hard, strike fast, but strike most out of love.
Cling to this day until its flanks are stone.

The Children

Not you, but what they made of you
is what they've taken
to shape their lives.

Not you, but some monster
who walked across a field in a golden sweater
while they trailed behind.

Not you, but a pair of eyes,
a wet flash of anger,
or some approving smile for some small thing they did.

You teasing or laughing,
skipping stones across some placid river,
back there in their minds.

Not you, but something in some other world
of their own making,
looking down on them—or praising

what they can't praise themselves.
You frozen in time,
the you that is not you forever theirs.

TWO

Everyday examples are legion. Just take the local main street. Is there a fabric shop or not? Many people have lived near a specialist outlet for years and never known it was there—until the day they needed just such a store and either are directed to it or spot it themselves. Afterward they cannot imagine how they managed to wander along that street so many times in ignorance of the shop's existence.

The User Illusion: Cutting Consciousness Down to Size
Tør Norretranders

Zen Living

Birdsongs that sound like the steady determined tapping
of a shoemaker's hammer,
or of a sculptor making tiny ball-peen dents in a silver plate,
wake me this morning. *Is it possible*
the world itself can be happy? The calico cat
stretches her long body out across the top of my computer monitor,
yawning, its little primitive head a cave of possibility.
And I'm ready again
to try and see accidents, the over and over patterns
of double-slit experiments a billionfold
repeated before me. If I had great patience,
I could try to count the poplar, birch, and oak
leaves in their shifting welter outside my bedroom window
or the almost infinitesimal trails of thought that flash and flash
everywhere, as if decaying particles inside a bubble chamber,
windshield raindrops, lake ripples. However,
instead I go to fry some bacon, crack two eggs
into the cast-iron skillet that's even older than this house,
and on the calendar (each month another oriental fan
where the climbing solitary is dwarfed ... or on dark blue oceans
minuscular fishing boats bob beneath gigantic waves)
X out the days, including those I've forgotten.

Intuition

It's not in your face. It says in quiet tones,
"I will help you."
It drives an ordinary car on ordinary roads
into the flames

no one else will see for many years. It listens
like a young man in love,
so far down inside a happiness
it moves pebbles and stones.

It wears its sleeves turned up above the elbows,
blinks in spotlights, cuts its way
through tripwires and English hedges,
delivers messages that glow

faintly as a low-turned halogen
lamp in the corner of a poet's bedroom. It
is deceptive
but without anxiety. It has

surveyed what it needs to know of farms and stars
and dismissed the rest. *"I will help you,"*
it whispers in doorways,
"I will help you, I will lift you up."

In Wyeth Country

In Wyeth country, where the Brandywine
Flows beneath rusted iron bridges, and in October
Each hill has a barn with white light shining through it,

And chaff swirls on the floor,
There is such calm
Waiting with ordinary faces by the windows,

It is almost unrendable. *Who commanded us*
To spend our lives in such slow work, to age
Long before we were ready,

To sit by these windows, hands in lap, and stare
At skies so blank of detail they could belong
To any country? In Wyeth country,

The house leans, the church is a shell,
Farmroads tilt into the fields and disappear
Like thoughts we follow to a ridge and lose

In other thoughts. *Brick. Stone. Wood.* And here
A plow in a furrow, a stump no chains could budge,
Glass broken from a smoky shaving mirror.

Rime Forest

That beauty near-death voyagers describe,
    returned to their bodies with heart thumps,
or try to describe before they realize words
    are to the eternal as the dark is to a lamp,

might be close to this, as if we've entered
    a mile long hologram of spiral nebulae
or the neuro-networks of a frozen brain,
    everything glazed and glistening, clarified

in a silence of hanging wind chimes, even the smallest
    twig an icy capillary, every millet blade
diamond-spined. Walk for a moment
    over the snow crust and the sound is stiff brocade,

the feeling slight gliding. Every reflection
    seems a further facet of a farther star,
and at the nexus of white galaxies,
    synaptic leapings in the sycamore,

ski trails down a broken milkweed pod,
    a crystal river through the interstice
of two larch boughs. Every branch and needle
    backlit by each other, Victorian lace,

chandelier pine cones, the last jet vapor trails
   crisscrossed in a fallen maple leaf.
Breathe slowly, look long. In only hours
   bedraggled life will reassert itself

and shaking melted colors from the sun,
   tend onwards as dawn. In a day or less,
mud and rocks and damaged undergrowth,
   the basal rosettes of the winter cress.

Ferns

Almost invisible, but once you look for them
nearly everywhere
like moss in crevices and drifting thoughts,

ferns are what it must mean
to love without yearning. Protectors
of everything small that needs to disappear,

deer mice and tossed trash, bad brushstrokes in a painting,
theirs is the softest name, the softest touch.
They are social workers

as social workers should be—so full of calm
even those who don't trust them
come into their care. Fiddleheads or not,

the rumor that once a year, on Midsummer's Eve,
ferns blossom with tiny blue flowers
and if a pinch of fern seed falls upon your shoes

you will be less apparent—this rumor
is baseless: ferns have tiny spores
that travel in dew and raindrops,

no more magical

than Henri Rousseau composing *The Peaceable Kingdom*,

or adder's tongues, cinnamon, wall rue.

In the world's secret corners,

men wish to vanish, but ferns are what look on,

trembling, holding all light green places.

Strip Malls

Even new, out on some leaving-the-city road
among the auto dealerships, small manufacturers,
and tool and die shops,
they always seem in danger of going under:
the tiny laundromat with no one in it,
Tony's Pizza closed, a few blue-haired ladies
in front of the three-aisle Rexall's;
the last gasp of the famous jewelry store
tarred and feathered, driven from downtown;
the ubiquitous bank with its tellers who have no last names
you've chatted up for years and suddenly they vanish,
swept away in a merger.
        Even when their parking lots are almost full
and teenagers lean about the Coke machines,
looking stupid as boiled carrots, as cool as fresh spit,
these strip malls, remember,
have, as Matthew Arnold said about the world,
"... *neither joy, nor love, nor light,*
nor certitude, nor help from pain." They were
conceived for profit, they'll go down for profit,
so ugly, so utilitarian, they'll leave
only in the mind the smudge of burning rubber,
a packet of Equal and a few McDonald's wrappers,
no torso of Apollo, no panther in a cage,
nothing about them inspired,
        no one who entered them changed.

Quiet, Quiet Now

As in crossing over the Bourne Bridge
    onto the Cape's curled lobster claw;
as in walking through a redwood forest,
    hands brushing the ferns;
as in the way mist clears from Crater Lake,
    leaving that hallowed blue of snow shadows;
as in the shade of regimental monuments
    off by themselves in Antietam's evening fields;
as in the middle of Kansas
    where all there seems to be is wheat and sky;
as in a glass-bottomed boat
    backing and idling over a coral reef;
as in the trapezoid buttes of Montana,
as in the holy woods of upper Maine,
as in the Storm King Mountain sculptures of David Smith,
as in the ghost towns of Idaho,
as in the Frank Lloyd Wright house where a black piano
    still hangs suspended over narrow stairs;
as in the light that falls into a Hopper painting,
    as on a porch in lower Michigan;
as how a memory of calm
    is like a tall and graceful woman in a summer gown
    standing on the porch, holding the screen door open....

The Simile

What it is like
is what it never is: a thing apart,
neither the joined nor what the joined joins to,
invisible love that nonetheless exists,
the almost but the never quite,
a yoking that, when seen, forever vanishes
into opposites. It's like
a faulty, although useful, rubber band
stretched between a finger and a thumb,
contains its own disclaimer and creates
its own sort of tension. It becomes
one and another and a third,
like the Christian Trinity or Buddha's hand
holding a pebble that is like the world
and once it is imagined it joins us
in ways no dogmatist could understand,
being caught behind fences, doomed
to the lie of the equal or not,
the lie of the either/or,
the metaphor
that's like a river crossing where a bridge has been blown down,
assimilation, war.

The Green Children

In the end I was so overwhelmed by the weight of so many
competent witnesses, that I have been compelled to believe
and wonder over a matter that I was unable to comprehend
or unravel by the powers of my intellect.

William of Newburg
Historia Rerum Anglicarum

They gave us beans to eat. Before, we ate nothing,
As we were unacquainted with the bread and water.
Of how we came here, I have little feeling.
There was the sound of bells and there were caverns
Through which we wandered long. The reapers found us
Near the wolfpits, and my brother struggled
Harder than I. He died a few weeks hence, his skin
Changing, but still green. Of better appetite,
I lived, I lost my color, and I later married
A man of Lynn, to whom I bore white babes.

I was lily-of-the-valley leaves, my hair
Like green moss by the brookside, and my clothes
Shimmered as the forest mist at twilight
So they burned them, thinking them bewitched. I chose
To speak but little of my father's house
But truth was, I remembered much. They claimed
We were of Merlin's Land, where no sun rises, falls,
Yet a brightness reigns. Child, did you cross
That river cast between us, asked a parish priest.
I did not, answered I, nor doubt the Holy Ghost.

Near Coggeshall, my brother's tiny grave. The grass
Grows thicker, taller there. Would that he lived
To relearn merriment. Sometimes I bring
My babes to play their foolish hide and seek
Among these tongues of stone, then hear the bells
Ring out upon the glebe. I do not understand
Why I was saved, what purpose brought me hence,
Nor do I care. I trust the Lord. I am content.
Let others hear our story and be mystified.
Green grow the rushes and the land is green.

The American Zen Master

Zen also is to be found, he tried to instruct us,
in a car dealer's showroom, and in shoelaces.... Also, in America,
you don't sit at the feet of the Zen Master
but you have coffee with him, preferably at Starbucks,
next to one of those outsized suburban malls where everyone
    looks half dressed,
half dazed and half dead. *"The secret of Zen,"* the Master said,
"may come halfway through a Yankee Candle store
when you realize you can smell nothing,
or from reading Hallmark Cards backwards,
or choosing nothing from an overstuffed refrigerator. But it isn't
    a secret."
                        As for our questions,
instead of smiting us around the shoulders with a bamboo cane,
he'd hand us little writing-intensive packets of Equal and
    Sweet 'N Low,
then lean back, smiling like a sushi plate. Sometimes, he'd babble:
"Tums, drive-up windows, ATM machines.
Checkout line scanners, 1000 Megahertz,
the industrial landscapes so remarkable." Often
we'd catch him staring at the intricate face
of a digital wristwatch, or contemplating
a simple button-down shirt on a white shelf in a Wal-Mart.
All things. *"Throw your computers into the eyes of children,"*
he loved to tell us. *"Work for the Federal administration,*
if that's what you must.

Wear last year's fashions, re-endure the 80s.

Take the last train to Clarksville.

If you meet the Buddha on the road, kill her." We'd come to Zen

because everything else seemed about the mystery, not of it,

and all we could think about for days was money,

Internet cable, huge pasta dishes. Our pain is real, we said.

The only words we have to describe our lives

are "Please wake us!" Our Zen Master

was patient. Our Zen Master assigned us these exercises: "Tie
  your shoes.

Open doors. Close them. Gaze

into the heart of a microwave. Fold a piece of paper eight times
  into halves.

Present yourself with the present." Still, we puzzled.

Riding Chevrolets into the dark, we'd turn around to find

only a series of accidents strewn behind us,

our dead mothers, our dead fathers, our dead friends.

And when he'd say *"Focus on what's in store windows,"* we could
  see the Obvious

and where the Obvious came from, and beyond the Obvious,

but the Obvious eluded us. I thought it was William James,

our love of Marilyn Monroe. He said it was the Suburu of
  Wiltshire Boulevard

and to give it more time. He didn't care. We shouldn't care.

No one should care. One evening,

he mentioned the greatest work is not to work at all.

So difficult. *So difficult to do nothing*

but gaze at the Momentum. The small boats upon the Momentum.

  We didn't get it.

We'd spread our wings and all they'd brushed was air.

He laughed at our earnestness. Finally,

when a man in a business suit, after only one interview,

grasped "the koan of the singing microphone without a voice
  behind it,"

smote his forehead and burst into spacious skies,

we became jealous. *"Here's your own koan,"* the Master
  whispered.

"Don't expect anything of it but itself:

'Why is the Statue of Liberty invisible as the scent of cherry
  blossoms?'"

then smiled his enlightened smile, and bowed off into Satori

or was that the Food Court, at the end of a path of blue tiles.

Cassandra in Connecticut

Some read what's left in tea cups,
Or soothsay cranium bumps, or Tarot cards.
I read leaf shadows on my neighbor's house
As morning sun brooks down among the poplars
Blown by a strong eastern wind. Here's Count Basie
Playing his piano. Here's a buggy ride.
And there's a wolf devouring a man of God.
But where's the kangaroo I saw two days ago
Leaping the Abyss? Where are the three grape clusters?
No matter. Now, in their repose, the shadows form
A Chinese painting of a cliff and waterfall
Gently serene. I climb among dark boulders
Until my neighbor's shape appears behind the screen
Door of his kitchen—and he walks out
Into a forest glade nine thousand miles from here,
Holding his cup of coffee, scratching his side.
                    I envy him
For what he does not see or need to understand
As deer cross his patio, flocks of morning larks
Shadow the face he turns up toward the sun.

April

"Catch me," she says, running faster
    than ever before, long sun-streaked hair
       floating behind her,
          long torso and long legs a blur,

"catch me!" It's April,
    warm from El Niño, with the dogwoods full
       of blossoms—April in the hills
          and April in the valleys. "Hell,"

she shouts, "you can't keep up!" He slows
    just as she'd predicted it would go,
       this race, this time.... Time flows
          backwards as her taunting fingers throw

him kisses when she pulls ahead, her slim
    body leaving him,
       then vanishing below the highway's rim
          he's barely reaching. I'm torn limb to limb,

he thinks—always coming to the meadow last,
    where she's always bending forward from the waist,
       panting, hands on knees but lifting up a face
          half-loving and half-pitying. "Some race,"

she manages. "You know I always win

    but you just keep competing, don't you?" In

        her eyes he sees the April wind

            stream past the boy he was when they began

this yearly challenge... April skies,

    runners' highs,

        the speed and glee of April and the mystery

            of why she's not once faltered so he can slip by.

The Selfishness of the Poetry Reader

Sometimes I think I'm the only man in America
who reads poems
and who walks at night in the suburbs,
calling the moon names.

And I'm certain I'm the single man who owns
a house with bookshelves,
who drives to work without a CD player,
taking the long way, by the ocean breakers.

No one else, in all America,
quotes William Meredith verbatim,
cites Lowell over ham and eggs, and Levertov;
keeps *Antiworlds* and *Ariel* beside his bed.

Sometimes I think no other man alive
is changed by poetry, has fought
as utterly as I have over "Sunday Morning"
and vowed to love those difficult as Pound.

No one else has seen a luna moth
flutter over Iowa, or watched
a woman's hand lift rainbow trout from water,
and snow fall onto Minnesota farms.

This country wide, I'm the only man
who spends his money recklessly on thin
volumes unreviewed, enjoys
the long appraising look of check-out girls.

How could another in America know why
the laundry from a window laughs,
and how plums taste, and what an auto wreck
feels like—and craft?

I think that I'm the only man who speaks
of fur and limestone in one clotted breath;
for whom Anne Sexton plunged in Grimm; who can't
stop quoting haikus at some weekend guest.

The only man, in all America, who feeds
on something darker than his politics,
who writes in margins and who earmarks pages—
in all America, I am the only man.

The Devotion of Thomas Merton

Without density, what is a poem, what is a life
but wind through the trees? Without snarls,
without a crowded race-car track,
thick rich bread or thick rich soup,
how will we be nourished as we work our way
out of ourselves? I've walked light paths,
I've lived in a bare cold room and wept
over a feather. When friends called my name,
I answered with silence. I forgot
books and paintings, history and stars
as single-mindedly, with great devotion,
I focused on a simple piece of thread
and one flower petal. But too soon,
I floated into God before God wanted me,
and became an illusion. No, it's density,
shadows, weight, name tags, tangled forests,
complicated maps of city streets
a poem must wander. Trains hurl
out of the darkness, disease finds many footholds,
crannies, and the mind's unguarded cells;
politicians football through our years,
wars carve and gut us. How can I
ignore the palaces, fun houses—all such cornucopias
spilling constantly? And yet, say scientists,
a pinpoint strand of DNA contains
all that ever was and is and is to be.

Yes, well.... Except relationships, the individual
relation of my pen against this paper,
the room in which I write, old mothy books,
my bell mobile, the traffic sounds and how
they're backgrounds for cicadas, how cicadas
bring back farms I've walked and these in turn
evoke Frost's poem of the boy who climbed
birches and then rode them down, and there's
a famous painting of a laughing boy. His hands
hold a mandolin. Gypsy music. World War II
death camps, the Enola Gay, the day I drove
a woman to a river, hills of Appalachia
tumbling like Zen—on, and on, and on, and on,
weaving layers, pushing buttons, building scenes
and piling blankets, tunneling in them,
carving, molding, giving, fastening
thought to feeling, feeling to the great
density of how we've made our lives
what they are now. And what is that if not
addition—every second adding to this heap,
this flashing glowing bundle of bright coals
we call ourselves? No, I can't go back
to a single lotus blossom in a silent pool.
I simply can't. Not if I wish to bring
the planet with me when my soul flames out
and I am with God, harvest of God's hands,
the changing echo bouncing back—into
the welcome of the ocean of God's will.

Memo from the Desk of Wallace Stevens:

Send me a postcard from
Chile or Tunis to
Tape on my dresser or
Sail through my office.

Let it be frightfully
Luscious or smashing for
Nightmares or psalm-sings and
Scribbles of pencils.

Find me flamingos and
Cats in the jungles with
Faces like moochers who
Thrust out their fingers.

Mail it from beaches where
Waves look like forestry
Ghosts in their gullies that
Waltz in the shadows.

Florida charms me—its
Keys with their looping toward
Cuba, their coral, their
Fishermen bronzing.

Yet, for my needs, if you're
Touring Morocco and
Chance by a view of a
Harbor or ruin,

Post it to Hartford where
I shall be waiting to
Sweeten the world with my
Blackberry mind.

Vehicle

Something for transport. A device
pushed or pulled or driven,
launched, perhaps. Paddled,
rowed across a river, flown
as out of JFK. Something that holds together
while being used: a train
racing a car across Kansas,
a bicycle, a motorboat, even
the Voyager Spaceship. Also,
the medium through which a thing
finds its way home: a novel,
the tenor of a metaphor,
a play, a role, a piece of music
used to display
whatever's shown off in it.... The oil
for mixing paint pigments.
The substance of no therapeutic value
conveying an active medicine: a poet
looking from a casement window,
the priest or rabbi holding a dying hand.

THREE

...there have been nights of no talk and nights full of talk. They are never sure what will occur, whose fraction of past will emerge, or whether touch will be anonymous and silent in their darkness.

The English Patient
Michael Ondaatje

The Familiar

We are all to ready to live with it: the nondescript
House on the barren road, trees of no distinction,
The colorless lake beneath the colorless sky,
So long as it seems to work. It has the
Force of inertia, the pleasures of talk
About weather. In its familiar grip
We can lie about ourselves and not be hurt,
Watch clouds hold level in a crystal ball.
But when it doesn't work, when dust
Blows along the road, the lake kicks up, the trees
Flail like the devil's paintbrush,
We hate it—whispering to each other
How dull we've become, how hideous
Your face, my face, our lutulent desire
To be and see and feel and know and touch
Never too much, lest we want more
Than stabs of love and momentary wounds
Healing so soon we soon forget they were.
        We were
Once strangers with our whole lives fit to tell.

On Roark's Farm

The day too beautiful to waste, the trailing arbutus
just under the snow,
we walked the rickrack cowpath by the old stone fence
—*how long ago?*

Long, long ago. Cardinals and early robins fled
our loud approach.
I think we sang; I think we must have said
—*oh, nothing much.*

The tattered fires that dance throughout our bodies
danced higher then.
We skipped and whistled underneath the trees
—*and kissed and ran.*

We found some yellow coltsfoot in an underweave
of mold and bark;
you made my fingers brush the cloven leaves
—*leapt from the dark.*

In the brief space of a meadow you stretched up
to grab the sun.
You peeled it, halved it, gave me it to sip
—*that moment's gone.*

But I undressed you, then I dressed you in the wind
until you felt
it negligee about you, how it swirled and thinned
—*when you reached out.*

Long, long ago—the day high-lofted kites
watched over us.
They rose up from the valley and their gangling flight
—*was rapturous.*

Letter to One Who May Be Dead or Not

I was woken this morning by a heavy wind
    unusual for summer, blowing the curtains
of the eastern window halfway through the room
    in huge flapping gusts

and lying beneath them, giving up on sleep,
    I thought of Wu Li's handscroll,
"Passing the Summer at the Thatched Hall of the Inkwell"
    and his long-absent friend.

What are you doing now? Do you still study
    mist in the branches and the way a stream
follows the easy patterns of a hill
    as it makes its way downward?

I remember the morning
    you decided everything was perfect
and were away for hours in the meadows
    gathering goldenrod.

And how you shut off radios
    with a snap of your fingers, saying,
everything about the world is now
    and needs no reporting.

How have you spent the years? I know
    money upset you. Does the light
still wash away your fingertips, the rain
    still remind you of monkeys?

As for myself, I'm what you might expect
    from someone who forever had his head
inside a book—a bit aside
    from the world and its bearing,

who, this morning, when he watched
    the curtains billowing, and the sun
leap everywhere that it could get before
    wind died and took it out again,

wished you staying here. Who else, in memory,
    could understand Wu Li, the clear
morning after rain, the quiet studio,
    those brushstrokes moving toward the paper's edge?

I got up finally. I drank
    my coffee on the porch and as I read
the morning paper everything I touched
    seemed held out from your hand.

Urban Pastoral

—for Lori

We're going to set up a new detective agency
in a *film noir* city—some building
with rickety stairs
and a neon sign out front. I want
an old black Underwood, a filing cabinet,
one of those rippled glass doors
through which the clients first appear as shadows.

The advertisements for ourselves will be
two lines in the Classifieds. I'll wear
a hat from the 1930s like my father wore,
you'll have frizzed hair,
adjust your nylons regularly
and bend far over in a low-necked blouse.

I'll be moody. You'll be tart. We'll blow
smoke streams at the ceiling fan.
The phone will be a candlestick that seldom rings,
but when it does, your answer will be long
and mine minimum.
Whatever comes, we'll take it on
in our different ways.

You'll work late. I'll stash
a bottle of Jack Daniel's in my desk,
lower right-hand drawer. Sometimes, we'll share,

but more often I'll get drunk alone
and fall asleep, my feet up on the couch.
Next morning, when you open up, I'll still be there.

Somehow, we'll survive: a missing child,
a husband's car left on an empty bridge,
wives wandering. I'll find myself
searching through the mansions of the rich
one day... the next
in the Father, Son, and Holy Ghost
walk-up tenements,

asking questions of the girl with weepy eyes,
the boy who sneers. For years,
we'll float the business on my old convictions
and your pluck. And who's to say
we won't be happy in obscurity,
and sometimes take the day off just for love?

And who's to say the case we're waiting for
will never come?
And if it does—the bag of stolen jewels
your quick thinking spilled, my knuckles raw,
my left side numb,
city hall gone up in flames,
flashbulbs popping in the corridor,

will we stay the same
or move uptown?... Enough of that. For now

I'll watch you polishing your nails,
you'll listen to me hum,
while on the fire escape, the petals will sail off
the red geranium

one by one. I'll read John Donne to you,
his Marlowe variation, and you'll tweeze
your eyebrows, tap your feet.
The nightclub of the city, like a feral cat
we glimpse and lure but never catch,
will leap beyond our sight
and jazz will merge into the milkman's song.

Sunday

—Race Point Beach, Cape Cod, Massachusetts

Benign, the seal's head bobbed among the waves
and at first we thought it the disembodied head
of a large dead dog, a Labrador retriever
or rottweiler, maybe. It disappeared,
but a few minutes later it was floating again,
less than a stone's throw from shore,
ugly, bobbing, calmly regarding us
as if *What were we? How did we come to be here?,*
the huge black nostrils flaring as it turned
ponderously, absent-mindedly, nothing of its shoulderless trunk
appearing before us. A few strokes out
and I believe I could have reached it if I dared,
despite the broaching tides, this part of the shoreline
rougher and deeper than others. It sank again
and for a long time all we did was stare
at the dark shapes of floating seaweed clumps,
shadows in the wave troughs where the wind
arose and abruptly died.... Until, *there*, just beyond
where the waves crested, in that back and forth
jellylike tipping and sliding seasick motion,
the seal's head once more broke the surface,
higher than us now, looking down upon us now
upon our small towels, who were kneeling, looking up
into the huge brown eyes of what we'd almost worshipped.

A Shadowy Government Agency

In the warehouse above us,
forklifts move huge crates from here to there.
The noisy business of the world goes on,
and no one's the wiser.

But down here,
everyone whispers. Even computers
speak with soft voices,
and if we hold each other's eyes too long

someone reports us. We wear kid gloves
even when dressing.
We tiptoe down the brightest corridors. We knock
before we enter

and step to the side, expecting anything,
wary of all. Sometimes we think of ourselves
as poets
adept at tracing odors of burnt rose. More often

we're simply fact-finders,
eccentrics,
odd ducks with a special knack for crunching numbers,
shy, silent people

who disappear next door to you with only a nod
on a warm summer night. What we love
is making plans, and then
step by step transforming them, disguising them

until what comes about
seems purely accident: that car crash,
that falling plane, that sudden heart attack,
the voice that amplified above the crowd.

These were our doings, I think. And yet
who knows?
None of us are sure exactly what we've caused
and what just happened. In our cubicles,

we dream of crows,
small paths running quietly through woods,
the secrets hidden in a field of Queen Anne's Lace,
someone to write our names on anything but water.

Some Man I Knew

Some man I knew, someone you should know,
stood here last night
under this awning. It was raining hard
and left and right across the street

people ran with papers over their heads,
some cursing, some laughing.
Bending ferns of water splashed up from the tires
of passing cars—this night scene a thing

Dufy could have painted well. The man
cupped his palm around a lighter flame,
sucked a sprig of fire into his cigarette,
and stood there smoking with such perfect calm

I swear he didn't care if he'd go on
or stay eternally. Shops closed.
What had been a stream of taxicabs
trickled down to those

few gypsy ones
you're never sure if you should hail or not,
and one by one the lighted windows in the high hotels
around him all went out,

and yet he stood there still,
when not smoking, humming to himself,
I think—the rain not letting up at all,
but falling like increasing wealth

so often keeps on coming to the rich
who have no need for it but like to watch
it grow and grow
until it's just a game of pitch and catch

and store away. Two hours passed. By now
the street had grown so dark, I wasn't sure
if I could stay awake. And if I nodded off,
would he still be there

who couldn't see me staring warily at him
from my dark room,
and even if he could, would never care
if I was safe or if I'd come to harm,

or even if I was. At last,
he put his hand against the rain
and with quick catlike strokes
splashed water on his face. I sensed then

the anguished look of one who waits and waits
far beyond reason,

the calm he had assumed so long,
for a moment, broken,

in the next, regained. Another cigarette, and finally,
head up and striding slowly toward downtown,
his shoulders never hunched,
into the pouring rain the man I knew walked on.

The Back of God

Is covered with whip marks, cancer cells; its muscles
Ripple when lifting weights. Dragon tattoos
Writhe on both shoulders. It is always turned
Against the righteous and the rich,
The meaty slabs of it cold and hard
As if just come from some gigantic freezer room
Or pulled from a river. The back of God,
Only slightly tapered to its buttocks,
Has no expression but what's read or gouged in it,
Is an awful blank stare, a cliff
Wracked with deep fissures. It's decisive
As a full packing crate, its spine
A series of spikes approaching an overhang
Impossible to traverse. Confounded by it,
Armies rage and die. Lovers beat their hands
Against its stiff flesh. It is the disembodied
Torso wedged between two generations,
The living carcass that you throw yourself upon,
Screaming and crying that it is not just
To treat you this way. In its huge shadow,
You ride the dark streets of your firm belief
That love's not charity and never freely given.

Animus

We plan our days, but our days have other plans;
The mood of one affects the mood of all,
As if the hours formed in caravans

Moving out, always moving out, a caterwaul
Commanding us to live our lives as theirs,
Seconds screaming minutes to nightfall.

We clothe our bodies, pad our earthenwares;
Lifting our hands, we shield our eyes from sun,
Anoint our newest journey with our oldest prayers.

This day, we say, there'll be no jettison;
We'll ford crazed rivers safely, top the hills;
We'll fat the meat around the skeleton.

But west skies darken; the good mind imbeciles;
A careless moment spins the frying pan;
New traces break; the mug of coffee spills.

What started promising becomes pedestrian;
The lead's been taken over by the also-rans.
We plan our days, but our days have other plans.

After a Proverb by William Blake

Every day, through lightning over the trees,
the television fog, through conversations
that never veer from malls and superhighways,
you must pull yourself back. Every day,
retreating across the board, watching right and left,
you must lift your hands to ward off evil,
and lower your eyes. The world's a mud hut,
a ring on the street, a stiff breeze blowing
through open windows of an empty Chevrolet.
Should you try to gather friends around you
and hold your ground with silken flags, with snipers
poised in doorway shadows, signaling one another,
a cardinal's wing becomes a martyr's leaflet,
a pond becomes a mirror; candles will turn
into the neon lights of shattered taverns,
jukebox reflections. Every day of your life,
remember that it's all impossible,
hideous, lovely, a Fayerabend maxim.
Hurt and murder are its sole taboos,
love its one calling. Every day, forgive
the weather of Egypt and the thought of Mars.
Touch her inner wrist so lightly she will shudder,
        court the outré.
A lily's to sip from, a sword is to wither.
Take a deep breath, and now a deeper one.

[Say We Have to Name the World Again]

Say we have to name the world again.
What will we choose?
I'd like to call it *Mystery* or *Castle*
and those who live upon it *Leaves* or *Water Droplets*.

But you, with your more somber tones, would name it
Grave in the Darkness.
You'd call breath *wishing* and you'd call the days
Pebble, Crow, Wind, Clock, Shoe, Mirror, Knitting Needle.

Say a plague takes us, say we lie outstretched
beneath *Nancy* or *Michael*
and the forest is *Wistful Feeling*, and that sound
is the computer, which has learned to feed itself.

Can you feel the majesty of Howard,
how sparrows fly through Nancy, Michael's hair is clouds?
Look down the raven, this is Pebble,
we are wishing rose scents in Old Mystery's arms.

If You Get There Before I Do

Air out the linens, unlatch the shutters on the eastern side,
and maybe find that deck of Bicycle cards
lost near the sofa. Or maybe walk around
and look out the back windows first.
I hear the view's magnificent: old silent pines
leading down to the lakeside, layer upon layer
of magnificent light. Should you be hungry,
I'm sorry but there's no Chinese takeout,
only a General Store. You passed it coming in,
but you probably didn't notice its one weary gas pump
along with all those Esso cans from decades ago.
If you're somewhat confused, think Vermont,
that state where people are folded into the mountains
like berries in batter.... What I'd like when I get there
is a few hundred years to sit around and concentrate
on one thing at a time. I'd start with radiators
and work my way up to Meister Eckhart,
or why do so few people turn their lives around, so many
take small steps into what they never do,
the first weeks, the first lessons,
until they choose something other,
beginning and beginning all their lives,
so never knowing what it's like to risk
last minute failure.... I'd save blue for last. Klein blue,
or the blue of Crater Lake on an early June morning.
That would take decades.... Don't forget

to sway the fence gate back and forth a few times
just for its creaky sound. When you swing in the tire swing
make sure your socks are off. You've forgotten, I expect,
the feeling of feet brushing the tops of sunflowers:
In Vermont, I once met a ski bum on a summer break
who had followed the snows for seven years and planned
on at least seven more. We're here for the joy of it, he said,
to salaam into joy.... I expect you'll find
Bibles scattered everywhere, or Talmuds, or Qur'ans,
as well as little snippets of gospel music, chants,
old Advent calendars with their paper doors still open.
You might pay them some heed. Don't be alarmed
when what's familiar starts fading, as gradually
you lose your bearings,
your body seems to turn opaque and then transparent,
until finally it's invisible—what old age rehearses us for
and vacations in the limbo of the Middle West.
Take it easy, take it slow. When you think I'm on my way,
the long middle passage done,
fill the pantry with cereal, curry, and blue and white boxes of
    macaroni,
place the checkerboard set, or chess if you insist,
out on the flat-topped stump beneath the porch's shadow,
pour some lemonade into the tallest glass you can find in the
    cupboard,
then drum your fingers, practice lifting your eyebrows,
until you tell them all—the skeptics, the bigots, blind neighbors,
those damn-with-faint-praise critics on their hobbyhorses—
that I'm allowed,

and if there's a place for me that love has kept protected,
I'll be coming, I'll be coming too.

Then

What came through the fields was a white horse
galloping toward us:
a white horse with red eyes,
snarls of black flies
swirling about it. What came
through the fields had blood on its mane
and blood on its forelocks—and blood
splattered its loins. We stood
watching it come. We said prayers
that it might swerve. We put our hands to our ears
to block out its whinnying.
We did everything
but run. A coven of sparrows rose
from the grass and settled again. Across
the fields lay the broken swath
of weeds its slashing hooves left
bowed in their wake. No god
to protect us! No road
of words we might take—the white horse
galloping across the fields toward us.

FOUR

Still, there are times I am bewildered by each mile I have traveled, each meal I have eaten, each person I have known, each room in which I have slept. As ordinary as it all appears, there are times when it is beyond my imagination.

"The Third and Final Continent"

Jhumpa Lahiri

The Cove

Something was out there on the lake, just barely
visible in the dark.
I knelt and stared, trying to make it out,
trying to mark

its position relative to mine,
and the picturesque willow, the moon-silvered diving board
on the opposite shore. I listened hard
but heard

no sound from it, although I cupped one ear
as I knelt in the cove,
wondering how far I should take this, if I should seek
someone to row out there with me. Yet it didn't move

or grow darker or lighter. Most shapes,
you know what they are:
a rock-garden serpent, a house in the mist, a man's head,
an evening star,

but not this one. Whatever was out there kept changing
from large to small.
The mass of a wooden coffin surfaced,
then the head of an owl,

a tree limb, a window, a veil—
I couldn't resolve it. I ran one hand through my hair
as I stood up, shrugging. I had just turned fifty
and whatever it was that might be floating there

I didn't want it to be. Too much before
that came unbidden into my life
I'd let take me over. I knelt again and stared again.
Something was out there just beyond the cove.

The Day Before Yesterday

It snowed, or did it rain? I think my parents were alive,
    swimming in Sacandaga Reservoir, the Adirondack Mountains
so around them that they seemed inside a crown
    as they splashed and they giggled. President Kennedy
was lifting John-John in his arms; a Peace Corps volunteer
    saw her first gazelle and a woman balancing a pail
of water on her head. Our son went off to college.
    Someone stupid was killing someone stupid for a stupid reason,
I wrote my first poem, I bought my first computer
    and when the screen went on an avalanche of numbers
jostled the future good. What I did is what you did and only
    the details are different. You unlatched a kitchen cupboard,
reaching into it to lift the sun and moon and stars
    glass from the others. On the Pennsylvania Turnpike
a Volkswagen flipped and slid; we saw a side door open
    into the sky. Time, as we know now, is relative
as the strobe light of friendship, the distances
    between intention and the careful consummated act
which may never come to be the way we have imagined
    clothes falling to the floor, a sparrow in the woodshed,
the rocket's red glare. Sorry. Wasn't that the day
    my brother found his cancer, my mother struggled hard
against the ambulance attendants who were lifting her
    up into Death? Didn't the telephone ring late? Didn't my father
lose the feeling in his hand? How the snow came down!
    Every plan we had went out the windows. Just TV

83

to soothe us into dreams.... I know I'm reclusive,
    a sleepwalker standing by a hedge at midnight
wondering why everything seems one remove away,
    muted, shadowed, muffled, soft, like having water stay
for hours in your ears; like looking through a veil
    at passing headlights on the street; like saying words
that move so faintly on the scrolls of reputation
    they might as well be wings I'm slowly painting
to make the margins less conspicuous. But here
    and there, I wake. Lemon chicken. Snowdrops. Stunning
phrases of Akhmatova, Dante, Catullus, Crane;
    pictures on six-sided tins of Earl Grey tea,
our gray housecats with their windowsill to windowsill
    endless tour of the house. Then I fall back again
into the dreamworld that is ordinary living,
    my feet and mind move by themselves, I can barely
tell tattered shapes of thought from mended shades of feeling,
    walls from ceilings, chairs from sofas, desks from chairs,
so dreamy life is. You say you are real? You say
    I hurt you? I forgot? I never sent that promised
letter of praise? On the day before yesterday
    fish fell from the sky, our daughter drew a line of blood
halfway down her arm. I lived on tranquilizers, lizards,
    every evening read obituary pages in my search
for notices that someone younger than I wouldn't walk
    the local malls or see the current movies....
You learned to drive. You cooked. You flew to Florida.
    Your mother tossed your father's ashes from the window
of a car in Miami's slums. Listen long enough to anyone

and you'll hear such stories—multitudes of them, and soon
the strange will seem the normal and the normal strange
    as a two-parent family, leisurely hours in bed
reading *The New Yorker*.... We were bound to Ohio,
    we were bound to Idaho, we leaned against a guardrail
above the Grand Canyon. You showed your small naked body
    off to thousands at a crowded nudist beach,
a boy from my college dorm became a name our fingers brushed
    on the Vietnam wall. We went to a poetry reading,
I misinterpreted a friend who meant no harm,
    angels visited a meadow in the dark. They danced
until the sky grew light. The Oklahoma Federal Building
    blew into the stars. Dying, say the women and the men of God,
is only displacement. Mystics say that everything still lives
    in the ash of a moment. What was is always mass
and energy: you're nothing, you are in-between, you're everything,
    cards being shuffled in the infinite dimensions
parallel to ours.... I was a sinner. *Save me.* I was standing
    by a road in upstate New York, expanding my collection
of license plates from all the country's states, but never found
    North and South Dakota. *Save me.* Save the smell
of cranberry bogs, mattresses on fire, straw and ice,
    Indian pudding, apples in the cellar, clover stems,
America's new cars. *Save the whales. Save the children.*
    Save the farmers. Save the unions. Save the feel
of a bellrope lifting you a half-inch from the floor
    and the mattering details, individual as each
moment is to any one of us, no matter what we share
    when the ball goes in the basket or the puck goes in the net,

the crowd comes to its feet and screams "Heil Hitler!"

on a Movietone screen. *Secret or horrible surrenders.*
You were the child with velvet eyes. You were the woman

marching for her rights. I hurried back to my office,
observing, recording, relenting. Silence has a way

of stopping history with a shrug, the white flag raised,
a corner nibbled from a city's skyline. . . . If you

believe in anything, believe that it is possible
when you look over your shoulder with that twist of head,

skipping yesterday, you find such swirls and knots and eddies
it is incredible we have survived our past,

an open perfume bottle on the mantelpiece, the tug of oars,
to be here wondering about what happened then.

Lost Friends

Where have they gone? Carol, who once exposed
   Her perfect body by the fishing stream,
Arms uplifted, rising on pink tiptoes—
   And then she dove

And disappeared from me. Donald, who read
   Descartes at seventeen and after that
Never took another book to bed
   But wed, instead.

Where have they gone? Where's freckled Sally
   Who wanted, more than anything, a house
With a tire-swing hanging from an apple tree
   So she'd be free

Of her mother's whining and her father's woes—
   Where does she live now? Where's Bob,
The baseball player with the upturned nose,
   Those splendid throws

That pinned the runners to his beck and call.
   Has he found happiness? Does Sharon still
Dream of dancing in a Broadway musical?
   And Bill, where's Bill

Who nightly loved to drive the county roads
     From Round Lake to Elnora,
Turning off the headlights of his father's Ford
     So I'd be scared

Enough to write, he said, of life and death
     With some intensity. We'd stop
At Jo Anne's house. Panting with relief,
     I'd catch my breath

And call her through the windows of the car
     To come and talk with us awhile.
Where's Jo Anne now? Is her long hair
     Still black, her stare

Still challenging? Where's Hank, where's Joe,
     Where's Lindsay, Joyce—and Dave and Gail
Who hugged a snowman in the falling snow?
     Where are they now?

Where have they gone? Is anything the same?
     Doris's fear of water, George's grin
As he explored rock rhythms with his set of drums,
     Weird Stanley's glum

Despair at getting anywhere, Marty's way
     Of carving little crying faces in his desk,

Our Eisenhower politics, our gray
    Fear of Doomsday?

And where am I? At sixty-one, I live
    Only slightly less half-hidden from myself
Than I did then. Some years, I've
    Barely survived;

Others, I've climbed around and shouted in,
    Doing my best to live a praising life.
Do they care or wonder in my lakeside town
    Where I have gone,

Or if I'm still around? Where's Claudette
    Who read my Latin on the schoolhouse stairs?
How we did declensions! The lives that we miswrought!
    Oh, *ubi sunt!*

Being Taught

Once a novelist showed me how a whole life might be caught
in a single brief sentence: *She was a woman*
who never walked in rain. Or, *Imagine a trumpet*
hanging from a willow branch. Creating lives, he said,
is half a game and half such desperate feeling,
it would be a mercy to go deaf and dumb and blind,
sometimes. *When he lit candles,*
he always thought of an Edward Hopper painting,
but which one it was, he could never tell his wife.
"Your life, for instance," he told me,
"how might you sum it up—or would you want to?"
If I lie in bed too long I feel my hands
will never stop shaking. "Japanese poets
do a similar thing with haikus," he said. "In fact
the whole of Japanese art can be explained
by mountain passes, butterflies,
robes left untied,
a swordblade misted with blood." We were walking
through a large Chicago mall
littered with cardboard. I watched a salesman
using only his left hand to tie a shoe, a girl
who swore at a mannequin as though it hated her
and all of her friends. *If I'm honest with myself,*
I'll disappear. He said every year or so
he had to concentrate on colors, blue especially,

the iceblue of an Adirondack lake
when it first freezes over, blue North Dakota ranches,
fishscale blue, the powder blue an evening snowstorm casts
in a car's headlights. But then he'd see someone
and the sentences would come again to him unbidden:
He was a man who loved to row dark waters....
.... Without intention, she dressed to be undressed....
All their houses smelled like smoke and beer....
He had a habit of shrugging more than normal,
as if a jacket or a cape upon his shoulders
would never quite settle. We stopped to eat
at one of those cheap steak places where they serve
catsup automatically with fries. Our waitress
hummed to herself and looked like she was biting her lips
even when she wasn't. *Animal, vegetable, mineral,*
which am I? Scissors, paper, rock. I looked around,
and all the faces, all the clothes beneath the faces,
the shapes and gestures of bodies
were turning into one line stories and I couldn't
stop summoning them, it made me dizzy:
all these lives that we were taking unawares,
confetti, heads of bobbing swimmers,
a sentence for each life. *Please, when mine is read,*
make it raw and beautiful at once.

       After lunch, we parted.
"Work," he said. "My work is a ship that sails away
and I'm on a wooden pier, hobbling, reaching out."
A boy at the bus stop corner glanced at him

vaguely... and I could swear that in this glance was how
the boy would see his entire life:

figures on glass surfaces, insubstantial, passing.

Jubilate

How many pale blue skies I've walked beneath,
Wildwoods and towns I've entered! I remember
Beaches and flowers, and children in the elms,
Mysterious sayings from the lips of strangers

That swept me for days from one path to another,
Sun on the wings of high white Piper Cubs,
A church door in Nebraska swung wide open,
The profiled faces in a thousand taxicabs

Skittering New York. Once, in the upper ribs
Of a valley at dawn, a field of Canterbury Bells
Rang for me. Once, along a lonely road in Maine
I heard the splashy turning of a watermill

Over a falls that wasn't there...and all
The books I've nubbed and underlined, the time
I slid down in a field to hear Bob Dylan's twang,
My first walk up the snail-ramped Guggenheim,

The trysts, the trinkets, meadows, baseball games,
Lakes, and river bays. I remember hugs and horns
At the end of World War II, and I remember
Every denim jacket that I've ever worn,

My first McDonald's, and the August afternoon
Nixon resigned. Sometimes, I think we're meant
To live our lives as gatherers of all the sounds
And sights and touches, tastes and scents

We happen on. Before the first brown moths
Come cluttering the window screens, I'll think
Of banjos, climbing ivy, New Orleans,
All the Buds and Michelobs there are to drink,

Freihofer's cakes to eat, rocks to kick, the kinks
And crazinesses I'll work some day out,
Cat Stevens singing with his head up in the sky,
This psalm of praise to turn my life about.

Letter to Ye Feng, His Student Now in Iowa

I remember your paper on the Tao,

How your eyes shone when you got each spelling right.

One late afternoon we talked for hours

Outside your dining hall, about the Korean War.

You wore your red nylon jacket all the time

To startle Americans, I think, although you never said so.

Americans are so possessed by things, you told me.

I asked, "And why do you so love your new computer?"

You were amazed when I showed you my worn copy

Of Mao's *Little Red Book*. You couldn't get over it.

When you got sick, you took a long train ride

Down to New Jersey, and an acupuncturist.

I scoffed, but he cured you. You said, "Look!"

And grinning, jumped up and down on the sidewalk.

One night you gave a party and respectfully

Listened to Bruce Springsteen as if he was classical.

You and your guests sat quietly translating,

Heads bowed, sipping your beers. I found that very funny.

At graduation, you insisted on having pictures:

Old American Professor with a Young Chinese

Student in Robes Beside Long Island Sound.

Now it has been a year. In graduate studies now,

You wear a white lab coat and study physics far away.

Physics are mountains to you. You ski down them.

You love the dawning of numbers, the beautiful flourishes.

Here, in Bridgeport, on our campus of a hundred trees,
Xi Ling, your friend, reminds me to say "Hello."

Poem for Li,
In Her White Bridal Dress

"How many miles to China?"
I ask my friend, the student Ye Feng.

"Ten thousand miles," he answers,
"it is always ten thousand miles."

"But how can I get there?" I ask,
"to be at your wedding feast?"

"Take to the river," he says,
"and then take to the sky."

"Where is your bride, Ye Feng?
Will she be blushing and young?"

"She stands at the doorway," he says,
"bidding her parents goodbye."

"Are there flowers around her, Ye Feng,
and lanterns, and gods of the night?"

"Feel the breeze on the mountain," he says.
"Hear bells in the dusk."

"Student Ye Feng," I ask,
"is China so far, far away?"

"Ten thousand miles," he answers,
"it is always ten thousand miles."

Texas Prison Town

"The only French he ever learned was *à la mode*
and went his whole life thinking it meant ice cream,"
she was saying. This was in a small green and brown diner
on the edge of Texas, on one of those spectacular Texas days
when it seems the wind will blow sweetly across your face
forever and ever. "Yessir," she said, "yessir,
he was some fixins." After a while, as we listened,
the talk at the next table veered accountably
onto Death Row prison meals. Last meals. *"Enchiladas!*
Guacamole, sour cream,
and draft beer so swirl-around-on-your-tongue
your whole body starts grinning." Another chimed in, *"No,*
steak and french fries, salsa on the side,
and for desert a shoot-yr-mama slice of yellow cake
with thick chocolate icing. Glasses of whole white milk,
and one of those little white-with-green-inside mints
as you roll out the door." And here we were thinking
Eggs Benedict, poached salmon, Neapolitans,
a spectacular Port, an ancient Chablis—forgetting
this was the edge of Texas where the warden sets
a twenty dollar limit from one local restaurant,
and allows you a cigarette, maybe.... The last three hundred miles
as we'd driven ourselves from New Orleans, life playing with us
its usual accidental games of random A.M. songs,
rest stops, glimpses of strangers' faces, chance encounters
with a cross on a hill,

gray dogs barking,

    city sunshine on an emerald ring,

we'd been talking of adjectives, how adjectives

can dull a noun down into mud, or sometimes

send it crazily spinning, as in *twisty* or *rampant,*

weather-beaten, chaotic, windstruck,

and turn a whole phrase into an advertisement for perfume,

an adventure,

or a dirge beside a river grave. The old cliché

footloose and fancy-free had been stuck in my mind for weeks now,

and *hither and yon.* . . . Our recent neighbors kept moving

because "we don't want this to be our last house," they said,

and every few years, my parents would buy a new car

"so this one won't be the last." Then there were

those caravans of silver Airstreams

we'd passed on the road, and big clumps of them

gathered on fairgrounds like cylinders of oxygen. . . . Philip Wylie

advised his travel-book readers never to return

to any vacation spot where they'd been terribly happy,

because they'd ruin it for good, rubbing off the gold,

dulling the palm trees, muting pavilion music. *Gears. Years.*

Proud Mary . . .

rollin' on the river. The object

is to let yourself loose within reason

and buttercups

and old computer monitors. . . . *"The Last Time I Saw Paris,"*

one woman pronounced. Her girlfriends chimed in: *"Save the*

    last dance for me."

"The Last Tango." "The Last Leaf." "The Last Goodbye."

"I wouldn't love you if you were the last man on earth."
"The Last Hurrah." "The last shall be first."
"Last but not least." "He who laughs last, laughs best"
and on and on they went. We paid our check. Outside
in a corral-like parking lot we'd never see again,
on a warm afternoon we'd never live in again,
being the people we'd never be again,
we watched the cars on the highway moving up toward Dallas
for a minute or two (we'd never know again)
and then joined the others, swinging ourselves into line.

Man of the Cloth

Right now, he thinks, right now a woman in Paris
is looking down upon the Seine and weeping
for her lost lover. She's just read *Madame Bovary* again,
Flaubert on her lips, those lovely syllables
half of church bells, half the dirge of rivers
and now, right now, her sorrow feels so deep
she almost knows God.... Thinking this
is like when one dream crosses through a field
of burdock, shepherd's purse, and meadowgrass
into another, one dream vanishes, the next
opens and a young man's walking Provincetown
on a deadly cold night, icicles like barnacles
under the windows of the closing shops,
and the streets are slipping curves. We are, he says aloud
(the man or the man in the dream, he doesn't know),
all bound to be failures, but what we've failed in,
love, pain, friendship, humor, courage,
whether it leans against a temple in the Andes
or shines on a secretary's bundle of familiar keys,
will be lost as the snow. Right now, right now,
a tree in the Himalayas tosses in the wind,
someone's climbing the steps beside Victoria Falls,
shoulders wet from the spray. A child of China
singsongs *Sesame Street,*
an eleventh cousin's poking at a fire, a daughter of Christ
kneeling and praying that the world be good to her,

and much more than a promise.... He thinks of Phil Levine
and Bernie Strempek walking through Detroit
toward iron furnaces. He thinks of seals' heads
cresting up through foam, another dream, this one
the semicircle of a mountain range
he's going to enter. He can see himself
from a bird's eye, a speck of consciousness
seventy miles in the distance as he travels
over and under and at last far out
until he blends into the landscape like all moving things
stilled in perspective, random, circumstantial
as a bit of rock, a spear of grass, a brief
disturbance on the surface of the Plains—and now
he puts on his collar; he adjusts it carefully
and makes his way past lilacs toward the church.

Although the Temporal Is Beautiful

No one prefers a halfway finished thing,
An apple left half-eaten on the plate,
The lukewarm eddy between love and hate,
A ball thrown lightly, a halfhearted swing.

When everything is neither here nor there,
What can I praise and what can I forgive?
All furniture is merely decorative,
The ballerina never floats on air.

I half-reformed my life. It fell apart.
You can't repair a thing left half-complete.
The half-constructed building down the street
Is not a case of ruin become art.

Houses left half-painted, days that can't decide
If anything but gray is right for us,
In their neglect become contemptuous:
We trusted them, and then they went and lied.

Still even worse are those who chat up fame,
Who love intending, but who work offhand.
They roll in plans like puppies roll in sand,
And when they quit halfway, the world's to blame.

The wars we hate most are the wars half-fought.
Left to themselves, they tanktread in our minds.
We're caught forever on their battlelines:
Korea, Vietnam—we're never getting out.

And so the ballad's grief will never end:
...*Half-owre, half-owre to Aberdour*....
I touched a wavecap with a flashing oar
And then went down before the rising wind.

Poem for My Sixtieth Birthday

From here, everything looks like Mozart's hands,
and barley fields. When I almost died,
gasping for breath in a red and silver ambulance,
I kept thinking the city was rushing over me,
one consequence of lying on your back and breathing oxygen
through a small plastic mask. Some months later,
I found myself buying book after book of paintings,
Georgia O'Keefe, Landscapes of the Nineteenth Century,
China in Art,
and didn't know why.... From here,
just beyond the ghost town of my fifties,
everything looks dizzy, as in one of those dreams
when you keep on walking out of enormous forests
onto beaches at dusk. Off in the distance
people or driftwood branches, you're never sure which,
seem to be waiting for a message
or waving to some of those sailboats running so far upcoast
they could almost be shark fins.... Sometimes, I catch myself
losing track of Time, relaxing to its wash, its sound
of sputtering oars and little snags and catches
from popular music.... *I found my thrill*
on Blueberry Hill.... Oh, how I hate to get up in the morning....
Three coins in a fountain....
But you don't know what it is, do you, Mr. Jones?
Afterwards, when I snap out of it, there's this

computer screen in front of me, and it's flashing

enticements and advertisements, links and nooks and crannies

from all over the world. . . . Those days in the hospital

during my recovery, I'd walk the corridors

and think of how religious was *Intensive Care,*

the dying man in the room next door to mine

terribly trying to control his daughter's life

right down to her last shopping trip. Elliptical thoughts.

Random feelings. . . . In a book or painting or a piece of music,

I like to find textures such as I might run my hands across,

a hidden cavern, a little joke

hanging by its tail in a shadowy cave,

some meadows, a crocodile, the footprints

of an old philosopher pursued by elves,

for it's the ramble I love, the nonsensical road

leading to the sensible one, or vice versa. The adventure

of going anywhere at all and not returning

the same person I was. . . . At sixty,

what's so amazing are the everlasting stairs, the raspberry bushes

and Web pages hidden in the dark,

cold wind on a warm afternoon,

sudden connections with the unexpected,

how much less you care about so much.

     And sometimes I can burrow all the way

from under my grudges.

     And sometimes I spend a whole day fishing for poems

in a little blue creek that runs down from the mountains.

     And sometimes I listen to Mozart,

stopping now and then to excuse myself from between the chairs
and step out onto the balcony
over the city, over the long barley fields.

The Litany of Disparagement

I

When I leave the lake unseen
And the willows weeping green,
The hills, the field, the ravine,
    Pray for me now and then.

When I envy friends' success,
My own life seems meaningless,
I hunch in my own wilderness,
    Pray for me now and then.

When snow lightly masks my face,
White pines are a blur of lace,
And I only quicken my pace,
    Pray for me now and then.

When I cross friends off my list,
Pretending they don't exist,
Caught in my past's trailing mist,
    Pray for me now and then.

When my children's voices are ice,
They hate my self-sacrifice,
How I turn things over twice,
    Pray for me now and then.

II

I drove, but I didn't turn.
I spoke, but I didn't learn.
I warmed, but I didn't burn.
   Pray for me now and then.

Cards held too close to my chest,
I loved the roads running west,
Old shoes and a leather vest.
   Pray for me now and then.

I never reached my floodmark.
The dog is a distant bark.
The tunnel whirls in the dark.
   Pray for me now and then.

The nurse bends low over me,
With hands and skeleton key,
She opens Death's mystery.
   Pray for me now and then.

Pray, for the willows must shake,
Ripples must die in the lake.
I am the life I forsake.
   Pray for me now and then.

This Far

for my daughter

Here, I leave you. There are tins of water
enough to keep you for a little while,
dried meat and biscuits by the pantry door.
Usually, the mice stay pretty quiet.

The view's not bad. Those are my favorite hills,
covered with pines. On a clear April day
you can see small paths among the boulders,
maybe an eagle if you're looking hard.

Try to remember that the telephone
is only for emergencies—may they be few.
Keep the doorsill swept. You can never tell
who will come riding up from the valley.

These are my books, a motley varied lot,
some too much read, some not much read at all.
If you want, replace them with your own,
or use the shelves for toys and flower vases.

You're going to be on your own—sometimes
for months on end. I've found it helps
to whistle frequently or make out lists
of foods you love and states you've traveled in.

The pump is just outside. The clothesline holds
two weeks of laundry if you're planning things.
Fasten garbage lids on tight. Little devils
come from the woods to forage every night.

I hope you like the sound of mountain streams,
by my count three. But I suspect a fourth
is somewhere out there. Every spring
I think I hear it flowing through the dark.

You might listen for it, too. But now
I've said enough, it's yours. And don't forget
I've left you butter in the blue and silver dish
and stubs and stalks of candles you may light.

THE AUTHOR

Dick Allen has received poetry writing fellowships from the National Endowment for the Arts, the Ingram Merrill Foundation, as well as the Robert Frost Prize for Poetry and The Hart Crane Poetry Prize. His books include *Ode to the Cold War: Poems New and Selected* (Sarabande, 1997), *Flight and Pursuit,*

Jon Gordon

Overnight in the Guest House of the Mystic (Louisiana State University Press), *Regions With No Proper Names* (St. Martin's Press), and *Anon and Various Time Machine Poems* (Dell). His poems have been selected for *The Best American Poetry* volumes of 1991, 1994, 1998, and 1999. They appear in many of America's leading journals, including *Poetry, The Atlantic Monthly, The New Republic, The New Yorker, The Hudson Review, The Sewanee Review, The Massachusetts Review, The American Poetry Review, The Yale Review, The Kenyon Review, Boulevard, The Gettysburg Review,* among others. He recently took early retirement from his position as Charles A. Dana Endowed Chair Professor at the University of Bridgeport.